DANCING WITH THE DEVIL

by Catherine (Cat) Crozier

First published by Dog Ear Publishing
4010 W. 86th Street, Ste H
Indianapolis, IN 46268
www.dogearpublishing.net

ISBN: 978-145750-400-6

This book is printed on acid-free paper.

Printed in the United States of America

THE STORY

This is a true story based on memoirs kept by Catherine (Cat) Crozier, executive secretary to NFL team Washington Redskins owner and "billionaire bully" Jack Kent Cooke, 1991 – 1993. It tells how she learns to tolerate Cooke's eccentric, bullying and abusive behavior as she struggles to fulfill her commitment to herself to keep the job for two years. The reader will be amazed how Cat, a young, vulnerable, nice small-town girl unwittingly winds up in the middle of the chaos and turmoil of Cooke's world and desperately hangs on as the daily emotional roller coaster races her to unimaginable heights and then suddenly drops her into the abyss of despair and chaos.

Every day there are new rules and she is regularly subjected to verbal abuse and forced to witness behavior that completely shocks her and causes her to question her sanity for not just quitting and walking out. She fights to hang on, desperately hoping things will get better and that she will find a key to unlock the irascible Cooke.

Dedication

To Charleen, your courage and grace blow me away.

FOREWORD

When I was 12 and someone asked me what I wanted to be when I grew up, I said I wanted to be secretary to the President of the United States (it was the 60's and, like most other young girls, I was in love with JFK). I guess you could say I came pretty close to my goal, if you count working for Ethel Kennedy, widow of RFK. But I'm getting way ahead of myself.

I grew up in a quiet little town on the Jersey shore in a close, loving, traditional family. I had one brother and three sisters and I was the middle one. My mother was a full time mom. She had a beautiful soprano voice and was a much sought after soloist for local and state choral and operatic productions. My father was self employed with a painting and decorating business and was owner of a local stamp & coin shop, the perfect outlet for his lifelong love of philately and postal history. He was also a dedicated mineralogist. Neither of my parents ever went to college and, though they were never wealthy, we kids were well provided for. Our Christmas tree was always surrounded by piles of presents and we spent every summer at beautiful Newfound Lake in New Hampshire.

Our home was safe and secure, on a quiet cul de sac and there were always other kids to play with. I was a tomboy in every sense of the word and was very athletic and competitive, traits I carry to this day. After one year of college, I married my high school sweetheart. After that short marriage failed, and being a "go big or stay at home" girl, I lived my life around my two major passions: horses and skiing. Through the '70s, I bounced back and forth between training horses in southern Virginia, living in the ski country of Vermont and working a "real" job in New York City to pay my bills.

At the age of 33, after my job as office manager of an economics firm on the 80th floor of Tower One of the World Trade Center came to an end when the company shut down, I moved to Colorado to be near the Rocky Mountains. I spent a year in Boulder where I took classes at the University of Colorado, and then I moved to Fort Collins to become a full time student at Colorado State University where I was accepted into CSU's first Equine Science degree program. It was time to get serious about my future. I graduated with honors and relocated to Maryland to assume the responsibilities of my first professional equine management job. A series of unforeseen events led me to Virginia and my job with Jack Kent Cooke.

Most people, when they return home at the end of a long, hard day at work, share their thoughts and frustrations with a caring, supportive spouse or significant other. At the time, I had neither. Except for a few very close, trusted friends and my family, there was no one I could talk to (discretion was required because Cooke was a public figure). After long, torturous days with Cooke, I would lay awake in bed at night and, in my head, defend myself and my actions and argue furiously with him. Unless I wanted to permanently give up sleep, I somehow had to get it all out. So I wrote. My memoirs were my therapy, my typewriter my therapist. The manner in which I was treated by Cooke was so foreign to me that I worked in a constant state of panic, fear and survival. My head would have exploded if I hadn't found an outlet. Every night, I sat at my typewriter and let my fingers run angrily and quickly across the keys. I couldn't get the words out of my head and onto the paper fast enough.

The reader is reminded that, during this time there was no email and cell phones did not yet exist.

CHAPTER 1

Yikes! How did I end up here?!?

I sat there, holding the phone far away from my ear, my face burning with frustration and my heart racing with fear, and listened while Mr. Cooke spewed his hurtful and uncontrollable anger at me.

"YOU JUST SHUT YOUR MOUTH AND GET YOUR STUPID ASS DOWN HERE WITH THAT ENVELOPE". Then another order: "YOU BETTER GET IN YOUR GOD-DAMN CAR AND BRING IT DOWN HERE. I'M GOING TO TALK TO YOU TOMORROW. THIS HAS GONE TOO FAR, MRS. CROZIER." Then "DON'T YOU BE SLAMMING THINGS AROUND ON YOUR DESK. . ." Then "YOU GET YOUR ASS OFF THAT CHAIR AND COME DOWN HERE RIGHT NOW".

No one had ever spoken to me like that! No one, not ever! I numbly gathered up the gray envelope, walked to my car and drove the 35 miles (in rush hour traffic) to Mr. Cooke's home in DC.

As I made the dreaded drive and waited in endless lines of backed up traffic, I wondered how in the world I had ended up doing what I was doing. My mind traveled back to a safer, saner, more peaceful and quieter time in my life which I now knew as "BC" (Before Cooke).

CHAPTER 2

Colorado: school days

My eyes focused on the mail delivery truck as it came down the street. It was just a few weeks before graduation and I was getting ready to go camping for the weekend up on Rabbit Ears Pass. I stood there and watched closely as the little truck pulled up to my mailbox and the mailman reached out to place the folded bundle into my mailbox. I waited another couple of minutes and slowly approached. I wanted to see what was in there but at the same time I didn't want to see. I was waiting for a very important letter.

Three weeks ago I scraped up everything I had to buy a plane ticket to Maryland to interview with an Arabian horse farm for the position of assistant breeding manager. I thought the meeting had gone very well and I returned to Colorado with guarded confidence. They had thanked me for coming out and told me I'd be hearing from them soon.

Four years earlier, at the age of 33, after working as a secretary and executive assistant (and part-time ski bum) for 17 years, I gave up just about everything to move to Fort Collins where I became a student in the Equine Science program at Colorado State University. I was determined to realize my lifelong dream of becoming professionally employed in the horse business.

When I wasn't in class or at home studying, I could be found at CSU's equine research center on the west side of town near the foothills, working alongside of veterinarians and vet students, learning everything I could about horses. It was what I wanted more than anything.

And now it all depended on the letter from Maryland.

I reached into the mailbox and carefully pulled out my mail. There was the usual collection of sale advertisements and other junk mail. The letter was there, in the middle of the bundle. Did I have my dream job? Or would I have to go back to the job ads? That letter was my personal five hundred pound gorilla.

I couldn't open it. Not yet. It was way too important to open in a parking lot. It required ceremony and a special place. I couldn't control what the letter said, but I would choose where and when to open it and find out if all my sacrifices and hard work of the last three years had been validated.

Annette, my much younger neighbor in the off-campus student housing, along with her pet guinea pig which was curled up and napping in her pocket, was over for our usual morning chat and coffee. I slipped the letter into my backpack and didn't mention it. I asked Annette once more if she wanted to go camping with me. She said "thanks, but I've got a lot of partying to do this weekend" to which I responded "ok, well, this old fart is gonna go find some peace and quiet and commune with nature. I'll see you later, have fun!"

I hopped into my old, reliable '74 Chevy Nova and headed west out of Fort Collins into the mountains to the beautiful lake where I loved to camp and fish and restore myself after a tough week of studying. The five hundred pound gorilla rode silently along side of me, stowed away in my backpack.

After a couple of hours, I pulled into my favorite campsite. I set up my tent, made up my bed and got everything nice and cozy. The next order of business was to get a hummingbird feeder set up. All I needed was a red Coke can. Thirty seconds of dumpster diving quickly yielded one. I carefully cut three holes halfway up the can, bent the still attached pieces out and rounded all the edges to make safe perches and feeding openings for the delicate little birds. I filled the can with the sugar water mixture I had prepared back home, threaded a string through the tab on top and hung it in a pine tree. Within minutes the ravenous hummers discovered it and I watched with delight as they fed and fiercely defended their precious new food source. I breathed in the fresh pine scented mountain air. The solitude and surrounding beauty was a welcome feast for my senses.

The letter . . . should I open it now? Not yet . . .

As the sun began to set into the distant mountain peaks across the lake, I took the letter out of my backpack and walked down to the water and sat on a big rock facing the sinking sun. It was time to open it and find out. I took a deep breath and said a little prayer. I slowly ran my finger under the flap and made a tear along the top of the envelope. My heart started to race. I slid the letter out, unfolded it and my eyes immediately found the words "we are pleased to offer you the position". I had so desperately wanted to see those wonderful and magical words meant only for me. My relief was indescribable. I jumped up and stretched my arms straight toward the heavens and shouted YES, YES, YES! I sat back down on my rock and let it all sink in. The job was mine, I had done it.

I studied hard, took my final exams and graduated with high distinction. Then it was time to pack up everything and move to Maryland to begin my life as a professional in the horse business.

CHAPTER 3

The short-lived dream

I arrived in Maryland at the end of May after a long, hot two-day drive shared with another CSU student and her two pet rats. Yes, that's right – rats! My life-long friend with whom I had trained and shown horses, Alta, and her husband Dave, had generously suggested I stay with them on a nearby farm until I got settled. I accepted their kind offer but insisted that I sleep outside in my tent as their tiny house really had no room for me, and besides, I needed my space no matter how uncomfortable it would be.

It was hot; it was humid and my work days began at 6 am and ended at 6 pm. Breeding season was over for the most part so I worked anywhere on the farm I was needed. I fed in the morning and evening and drove the farm's ancient pickup into all of the different pastures while other crew members opened and closed gates and tossed the hay into the mangers. We cleaned the stalls in all of the barns and outbuildings. I assisted the vet whenever she came to the farm and I hauled horses when necessary. And, finally, I assisted the breeding manager with what little work needed to be done in the lab and breeding barn. Worst of all, I had only one day off each week.

Every night when I got home from work, I was covered with dirt and hay dust. I had sweated away 20 lbs in just six weeks. I was exhausted. My single days off were over before I knew it. I had no time for a social life. I had no time to visit my family in New Jersey. And I was sleeping in a tent because I wasn't making enough money to afford a place to live. It all wore me down and I grew more and more discouraged. I started to doubt myself and my career choice.

The best experience I had had at the farm was to help a young mare foal for her first time. I would never forget the look of amazement on her face when, after she had delivered a beautiful healthy foal, she lifted her head and looked behind her to see what all the fuss had been about.

But it wasn't enough to keep me going.

Finally, one day, I said to Alta "I don't know if I can keep on going like this. Now I know why this job is really for the 20-somethings and not the 30-somethings. It's all just become so hard, I don't know if my heart is in it anymore." Alta, always supportive, responded "Hey kiddo you know that whatever you decide, I'm right behind you. You're always welcome here, you know that."

I had to face reality and make a new plan. A few weeks later, I gave notice and walked away from the career I had dreamed of and worked so hard for. I would have to fall back on my trustworthy, ever faithful executive assistant profession. I was starting all over again.

CHAPTER 4

Washington DC: back to square one

I called my friend, Hal — a former boss from my New York City days — who was now in the Washington DC office of KPMG Peat Marwick and asked him if there were any openings at his office. I couldn't believe it when he said "I'm really glad you called me because my assistant is leaving. How soon can you start? Why don't you come down and spend the weekend with Rosalie and me and I'll drive you around and show you the area and maybe even look at some places where you could live." Wow, what luck! I quickly responded "Thanks Hal, I'll see you Saturday."

I moved to the DC area and spent the next couple of years working for Hal. I settled into one of the northern VA suburbs, where I rented the lower level of a townhouse. The ripe old age of 40 was staring me in the face. My biological clock was ticking louder and louder. I was lonely. My social life was nonexistent (where were all the men?) and I wanted my own home so I could have a cat again.

In spite of the joy of working with Hal again, my life was empty and lonely and without focus. I mean, let's face it, work by itself wasn't gonna cut it. I often found myself wondering why there was no "lid" for this "pot". I was a pretty cool person; I had lots of good qualities and interests and lots to offer. Maybe I just hadn't stayed in one place long enough. I tried expanding my social circle by becoming a volunteer at the National Zoo. I also tried joining different special interest groups. The single guys I met weren't fit for social consumption! I remembered something a girlfriend from Alaska once said about the guys there: "the odds are good that the goods are odd". Oh man, if that wasn't the truth! It wasn't that I was a snob, I wasn't looking for movie star looks or a Rockefeller, I was just looking for nice guy to do things with. He didn't exist!

On my 40th birthday Hal & Rosalie threw an elegant surprise dinner party for me at the Tower Club in Tysons Corner, VA. When I walked into the room (dateless) and looked upon the smiling happy faces of my new Virginia friends (all with their spouses or significant others), I decided it was time to take control of my life instead of wait for it to happen to me. Within one month I moved into my own apartment in Ashburn, Virginia (a little further west from DC where rents were lower) and went straight to the local shelter and rescued a precious, hyperactive five week old tabby kitten whom I named "Dickens" because he was so full of the dickens. Life for me was already improving by leaps and bounds. My (key word was "my") apartment was a wonderful refuge for this privacy-hungry girl and her new little feline companion. It was brand new construction and I was on the top floor. My backyard was beautiful woods full of singing birds and all sorts of other little woodland critters.

Soon after I moved to Ashburn, Hal called me into his office and said "Cat, I'm leaving Peat Marwick. The President has asked me to come to work for him. I can probably find something else here for you if you're interested." I accepted the secondary position at KPMG with the understanding that I would start looking for a job somewhere else. I couldn't believe it; I was back to square one again! I was happy for Hal and his good fortune, but what about me? What in the world was I going to do now? I just didn't seem to fit in anywhere.

I wallowed in self pity for about an hour and then I shook it off and refocused all my energy on finding a new opportunity. Something good was out there and I was gonna find it. I was a survivor – not a victim – and it would take a lot more than this to knock me down. (Looking back and considering the enormous challenges that lay ahead of me, this was very prophetic.)

CHAPTER 5

"Private individual seeks executive secretary"

A couple of weeks into my job search I ran across a simple four line ad in the *Washington Post*: "Private individual seeks executive secretary; respond PO Box XXX, Middleburg, VA". My heart and my mind started to race as I read between the lines. Middleburg meant horses; it was prime Virginia hunt country. In a flash I pictured myself working as an executive assistant on a beautiful horse farm in Middleburg. Wouldn't it be wonderful, I thought, if I could get horses back into my life and be an executive assistant at the same time. I eagerly cut out the ad and responded right away.

A few days later, I got a call from the "individual's" representative and was asked to come to Middleburg to interview for the job. I still did not know the name of my prospective boss. I had always enjoyed driving out to Middleburg and looking around in the quaint little specialty shops, though most of what they carried was way out of my price range. I drove through the town and started winding my way to "Kent Farms" the name of the "individual's" estate. I drove past acres and acres of incredibly beautiful, rolling green pastures bordered with New England style stone walls. Each farm was anchored by the obligatory huge country estate home. Finally, the entrance to Kent Farms came into view and I turned in. The driveway seemed to go on forever and disappeared into trees and perfectly manicured grounds. It was a pathway of the wealthy and privileged that screamed to intruders "ARE YOU SURE YOU BELONG HERE?". "No trespassing" signs weren't necessary here.

After following the driveway for what seemed like miles, I came to the small office building where I was to be interviewed. It was a small, no-frills, pre-fab type building. The "individual's" house was not visible. I parked my car and entered the building, was greeted by an office assistant and waited for my interview. I didn't have to wait very long, but during the short time I sat there, I noticed how little the people interacted with each other, and how carefully and sparingly they used their words, as though they had to pay a price for each word spoken. I also noticed they carried out their various tasks and duties in an almost military like fashion in that every action was intentional and that no time or motion was wasted. It was not a place filled with happy, normal people. On the contrary, it was a place where it seemed like everyone was being watched all the time. Little did I know…

I was soon greeted by the manager and I followed her into her office where she asked me the usual sort of interview questions. Once she had satisfied herself that I was serious interview material, she proudly announced to me the "individual's" name: Jack Kent Cooke. Keeping her eyes on me, she leaned back in her chair and waited for my reaction. She had presented the name as if she were placing a 24 pound perfectly roasted Thanksgiving turkey on a meticulously set table. If ever there was a pregnant pause this was it. I was in a total panic. The name didn't ring a bell! I had absolutely NO idea who this man was! I thought to myself "OK, well, I sure blew this one. Way to go Cat!" Not being much of a football fan, I barely even knew who the Redskins were and I certainly hadn't lived in the DC area long enough to know who the owner was. After a very long and awkward moment of total silence, I couldn't believe it when I realized she was actually pleased with my ignorant reaction. She explained to me who Mr. Cooke was and told me he was a billionaire. She gave me a quick rundown of his holdings, most visible of which were the Washington Redskins, the Chrysler Building in New York City and Elmendorf (race horse) Farm in Kentucky. She told me Mr. Cooke had previously owned the LA Lakers, the LA Kings, The (LA) Daily News and that he had built The Forum (also LA).

She told me that if I got the job, I would work in Mr. Cooke's home in Washington DC where he lived with his wife and two stepsons. My head still spinning from all I had just heard, I answered the rest of her questions and was sent down the hall to take the obligatory typing and shorthand tests. The meeting and tests completed, I was thanked for coming in, told they'd be in touch with me, and sent on my way. "Yikes", I thought to myself on my way home, "what am I getting myself into?"

I didn't have to wait very long to hear from them. The next day I received a call from Cooke's representative and I agreed to drive to Mr. Cooke's home in Washington DC to be interviewed by him. I had made the first cut. The representative spent at least ten minutes giving me directions to the house and also step by step directions for calling from the gate, which door to go to, how to announce myself, etc. She had left nothing to chance. I thought that was a little odd but soon forgot about it.

Carefully following the idiot proof directions, I threaded my way into DC and up Rock Creek Parkway to DC's affluent northwest section and, finally, onto the street where Mr. Cooke's home, "Marbella", was located. I pulled up to a big wrought iron gate, anchored by stone pillars. Inside the gate, the spacious driveway/parking area was paved with gray stones set in a wavy pattern. And there was Mr. Cooke's "Marbella", his Washington DC residence. It was a spacious modern style home which reminded me of a home that would have been designed by Frank Lloyd Wright on a good day, surrounded by two or three thoughtfully manicured acres. The land in front of the house had been landscaped to look like a natural area and even had a man-made babbling brook. Also in the front yard was a small in-ground swimming pool surrounded by a spacious patio.

As directed, I pushed the call button on the gate and identified myself to the answering voice. The gate opened and I drove inside and parked my car. I was met at the front door (I didn't know then that this first front door entry was to be my last) by a black servant dressed in a white house jacket and wearing slippers. He had a big smile and very friendly face. He politely asked me to remove my shoes because of the marble floor. I thought "hmm, this is sort of weird, could they be Buddhists or Hindus? What if I have to run for my life?" I half joked to myself. But I figured what the heck and took off my shoes. I was secretly relieved that I was wearing opaque stockings so no one could see how badly I needed a pedicure. I stepped onto the sacred marble floor and entered the formal living room. There were antiques everywhere and very formal chairs and sofas. It was cold and uninviting, not the sort of place I could ever feel cozy and comfortable in. Shoeless, I followed the servant to the doorway of the library where my presence was announced. It's show time, I thought to myself.

Mr. Cooke was seated at a huge antique partner desk. He was a short, slight man with longish silver hair and sparkly blue eyes. Though he was not a large man, he had the commanding presence of a giant. He stood up, presented a hand gnarled by arthritis and warmly welcomed me. He told me to sit down in the chair on the opposite side of the imposing desk. He was very charming. He got right down to business and candidly and quickly told me he was the owner of the Washington Redskins, the Chrysler Building in New York City, Elmendorf Farm in Kentucky, and many other properties. He asked me a few questions about my background and interests and suddenly, almost in the same breath, offered me the position. When I tried to find out the specifics of the job, he was intentionally vague.

I had never worked for anyone famous before and, my curiosity overwhelming my common sense and blocking the frantic messages my gut was sending me, I threw caution to the wind and ignored all the subtle warning signs (the odd behavior of Cooke's staff at Kent Farms, the no shoes on the marble rule, the hasty job offer) and accepted the job. In retrospect, Mr. Cooke's swift offer and closure of our "deal" was very characteristic of the way he did business. If it turned out he was later unhappy with the deal, he'd just terminate it, simple as that. He was always completely in charge.

Ah, ignorance is bliss! I was so excited about my new job I called Hal, I called my parents, I called Alta, I called my sisters, I called everyone!

I thought about how good this job would look on my resume – something I badly needed in light of my recent disasters. I made a vow to myself that I would keep this job — no matter what — for two years.

If only I had listened to all those little alarms and warnings that had gone off in my head! Little did I know that I had just committed myself to the two most difficult and challenging years of my entire life.

CHAPTER 6

Have you got a passport, dear?

It was my first day of work, just a few days before Thanksgiving 1991. There was no need for my alarm clock this morning. As usual, my cat Dickens was gently caressing my cheek with his big soft paw, silently willing me to get up and feed him. After I fed Dickens and scooped his "love nuggets" from the litter box, I hopped into the shower. I made the 25 mile drive into DC, along with what seemed like half the population of Northern Virginia, and threaded my way up Rock Creek Parkway to Marbella. I arrived shortly before 10 am, my agreed upon starting time. I parked my car on the street (now that I was an employee, my car was no longer welcome inside the property), entered the code which opened the gate, entered the garage and knocked on the kitchen door. Mr. Cooke's cook cheerfully greeted me and invited me inside. He reminded me to remove my shoes and explained that Mr. Cooke allowed no one — except himself and Mrs. Cooke — to walk on the marble floors in their shoes. I made a mental note to bring slippers to work.

The cook led me through the living room and the library and into what was now my office. It was a very plain, undecorated room painted in standard construction white; it reminded me of a room where one of the servants might sleep. There was a desk, a telephone, a typewriter, a fax machine and a paper shredder. On one side of the room was a shallow closet of shelves that ran the length of the wall, in which there was a personal safe, office supplies and an assortment of Redskins shirts and hats that Mr. Cooke kept on hand to give to friends and visitors.

There was no one there to train me, not even my predecessor, for just one day. I was on my own. I would soon learn that this was because no staff members were allowed to talk to each other, other than to conduct necessary business. I would have to learn Mr. Cooke's ways of doing things the hard way: by trial and error. Also, no one told me there were rules – lots of them. I only learned about them when I broke them and, believe me, I never broke them again. Breaking one of Mr. Cooke's rules was a painful experience and one that I would not soon forget. Some of the rules were:

- There were four possible answers to Mr. Cooke‘s questions: "yes sir", "no sir", "yes Mr. Cooke", "no Mr. Cooke".
- There was only one possible response to Mr. Cooke‘s incessant rantings and unfounded accusations: "I'm sorry sir".
- There was to be no use of first names amongst employees. For example, I would address my co-workers as Mrs., Mr. or Miss X.
- Mr. Cooke‘s most recent ex-wife, Suzanne Cooke, mother of their young daughter Jacqueline, must always — without exception — be referred to as "The Bitch", especially when mentioning her directly to Mr. Cooke. No one was allowed to say her name.
- Never try to defend yourself to Mr. Cooke.
- Never, ever defend the actions of other staff to Mr. Cooke.
- While at Marbella, shoes off! Slippers only to be worn on marble floor. The only exceptions: Mr. & Mrs. Cooke and VIP guests.

Mr. Cooke had not yet emerged from his bedroom. I hung up my coat, opened my briefcase and set out my tools of the trade (favorite reference books, calendar, etc) and waited for Mr. Cooke to "arrive" for work. Eventually he made his way into the library, greeted me as if I had been there for years and sat at his desk. I sat quietly in my office and waited for him to call me.

After a short while, he called me into the library and asked me if I had a passport. I had never traveled out of the U.S. so I didn't have one. I replied "no sir". Without hesitation and without saying one word to me or explaining what he had in mind or even asking me if I had plans for Thanksgiving, he picked up the phone and called the Secretary of State's office and explained that he and Mrs. Cooke were traveling via his private jet to his home in Acapulco, Mexico for Thanksgiving and that his personal assistant (me!) needed a passport RIGHT AWAY because she was accompanying them.

I thought to myself "what, are you crazy? Did it ever occur to you that I might want to spend Thanksgiving with my family?" But it was my first day and not wanting to ruffle any feathers, I didn't say a word.

Within minutes I had a special appointment at the passport office to fill out paperwork to be used for expedited issuance of my passport. It was quite an introduction to the kind of power this man was capable of wielding. Off to the passport office I went and I soon returned with passport in hand. What next? I wondered.

At 6 pm, I left Marbella and drove back to Ashburn, again accompanied by that same half of the population of Northern Virginia. I was still trying to wrap my head around what had happened that day. I had had a passport issued within hours by the Secretary of State's office and I had been told I was flying to Acapulco for Thanksgiving on a private jet. And this was only my first day!

My faithful little Dickens was waiting for me when I got home. I opened the door and there he was, his friendly little face looking up at me, saying "hi Mom, what's for dinner?" As I held him and he nuzzled his warm furry head against my cheek, purring loudly, I left the challenges of the day behind and began to relax.

But I still had to pack for Acapulco! There were just two days until we left, so instead of going for my usual bicycle ride, I dragged out the tired, worn out summer clothes I had just packed away and sorted through them. What did one wear on a private jet anyway? After what seemed like hours of inspecting, rejecting and selecting various blouses, tops, shorts, skirts, etc, I finally gave up and crawled into bed. 7 am rolled around before I knew it.

As I stepped into Marbella's kitchen that morning, the cook told me the trip to Acapulco had been canceled because Mr. Cooke had fallen and had a bruise on his face and he didn't want anyone to see it. I was a little bit shocked and disappointed at this because of all the trouble and hassle I was put through yesterday to get my passport and then pack for the trip. I thought and was hoping that maybe the cook had got it all wrong and that the trip was still on. After all, I had never been on a private jet and was looking forward to the experience. I didn't see Mr. Cooke that day, however, and other house staff told me that Mr. & Mrs. Cooke had had a terrible fight in the kitchen which apparently resulted in the canceled trip (and maybe the suspicious bruise on Mr. Cooke's face?).

I was quickly learning that this job was going to challenge me every day in ways I never would have imagined. I would also soon learn that while Mr. Cooke may have been very much in control of the business aspects of his empire, he had little control over his personal life; in fact it was often in shambles. I had yet to meet the notorious 4th Mrs. Cooke, the "Bolivian Bombshell" who had her husband tightly wound around her little finger and, with little effort, could reduce him to a total fool.

As I made my commute home that night, I began to wonder what I was in for, working for this man. I didn't know it yet but this was going to be the wildest roller coaster ride of my life. A journey that would be exhilarating one minute and torturous beyond belief the next.

So, that night, the summer clothes went back into storage along with the new VIP passport. There would be no trip to Acapulco on a private jet for me.

The next several days passed without incident. The Redskins were winning like crazy and the excitement for a return trip to the Super Bowl was reaching a fever pitch. Mr. Cooke was a huge celebrity everywhere he went and he soaked up all the adoration and attention like the Kalahari Desert in the first monsoon of the season. All was well and he was a happy man.

And I finally met Mrs. Cooke. She had stopped shopping long enough to come home. She was polished from head to toe, her long, dark brown hair was freshly coiffed and she was completely dressed in couture. She had a beautiful figure and she was stunning. She was sitting in the library with her little white poodle, "Chanel", in her lap and having a glass of wine with Mr. Cooke and some hors d'oeuvres the cook had prepared for them. Mr. Cooke was completely gaga around her. He couldn't take his eyes off of her. I went into my office and closed the door to give them privacy.

CHAPTER 7

Curmudgeon

It was about ten days before Christmas and Mr. Cooke was in high spirits. He was joking around with staff, calling me "dear" and having fun. The houseman came into my office and placed the mail on my desk. I sorted through it, got rid of the obvious junk, put Mr. Cooke's letters in a folder and set it on his desk. I then sat down on the opposite side of the desk and waited for him to review the letters and dictate his responses. There was one fan letter from someone who claimed to be an "old friend" of his. He looked at me, amused, and exclaimed "I don't know this person, I've never met him." He held the letter and, after pondering it for a few moments, dictated a response which began in a very dramatic tone, "Dear Old Friend". After he finished the flowery letter he looked up at me with a big smile and those crinkly blue eyes and said "how about that for a letter to my 'old friend'?" We both laughed. When he was like this he was such a pleasure to be around. He could really be likable when he wanted to be. I wished he could be like that all the time; it would have been so much easier to work for him.

There was also a letter that day for Mrs. Cooke – a chain letter from a total stranger that promised a lot of money if she forwarded it to 20 people. Mr. Cooke directed me to go through the phone book and randomly select 20 people to send the letter to. Wow. I couldn't get over the fact that a billionaire would waste his time on such a silly thing! I finished the 20 letters and wondered what I would be asked to do next. The rest of the day passed uneventfully.

CHAPTER 8

A discussion about the word 'fair'

About a week before Christmas I needed to go to the post office to mail a package to Bolivia for Mrs. Cooke. I went to Mr. Cooke and told him I needed money to mail the package. He asked "how much do you want?" Not having the slightest idea, I said "oh, it'll probably be a fair amount". He immediately cut me off and demanded that I give him an exact amount, saying that a "fair" amount was not an acceptable answer. How the hell was I supposed to know? I didn't have a postage meter or weight scale. He handed me a twenty dollar bill and said "be sure to come back in FAIR condition" and "be sure to come back in a FAIR amount of time". I bit my tongue and didn't say a word and went off on my errand.

When I returned from the post office, Mr. Cooke was proudly showing off the antique Persian rug he had recently purchased at a Christie's auction and which had been laid down in his office. He was in a jovial mood and asked me how I liked the rug and what did I think of its present location next to his desk (as if my opinion really mattered). I looked at him thoughtfully and replied "oh, I think it looks pretty FAIR there, Sir". He offered no response so I smiled to myself and returned to my office. Ever the optimist, I looked for every opportunity to try to form some sort of bond with the recalcitrant old man.

CHAPTER 9

Merry Christmas, Miss Crozier

It was a few days before Christmas and the daily mail packet from Kent Farms had been delivered. In it was an envelope containing Christmas bonus checks for the Marbella staff. Though I had only worked for Mr. Cooke for one month, I was hoping I'd get something. After all it was Christmas! I gave the envelope to Mr. Cooke and he had me assemble the staff in the library. As I stood alongside of him, he ceremoniously presented the bonus checks to the housekeeper, the cook and the houseman. There were no envelopes left. He looked at me and simply said "You just haven't been here long enough, dear".

I kept my disappointment and humiliation concealed and acknowledged his terse comment with the only acceptable response, "yes sir", and returned to my office where my mind ran wild with my thoughts. How could he do that? How could he, or anyone for that matter, be so thoughtless and cheap? I was so shocked, I just couldn't understand it. I was a very generous person and I didn't understand Cooke's total lack of consideration. I felt like I had been slapped in the face. "Merry Christmas to you too Mr. Cooke", I said to myself, and got on with my work. I couldn't wait to get out of there and away from the old miser.

CHAPTER 10

You won't find the better life here

Christmas had come and gone in a flash. I made a quick trip up to New Jersey to spend the holiday with my parents. I had appeared at their door tired, my spirit on the verge of being broken, a casualty of the Jack Kent Cooke Demolition Derby. My wonderful parents gave me the unconditional love and emotional support I so badly needed. They listened patiently as I described all of the unbelievable events and behaviors I had had to deal with day in and day out.

I was only five weeks into my job and I was becoming frantic, trying to come to terms with what I had gotten myself into and wondering if it was going to turn into yet another ugly smudge on my resume. I desperately wanted to keep the commitment I had made to myself to stick it out for two years with this crazy man. Two years! Five weeks had almost done me in. How on earth was I going to survive two years? I didn't want to become road kill on the Jack Kent Cooke Highway. I had to be strong and somehow turn my skin into teflon so that anything Cooke did, no matter how humiliating or unkind, would just bounce right off me and not upset me. It was the only way I was going to get through this. Fortified by lots of hugs and love from Mom and Dad, I returned to Virginia with renewed determination to succeed.

Soon after I returned, the houseman made an innocent mistake in performing one of his duties and he had come to me for advice on how to make it right. The problem was easily fixed and no harm had been done. Unfortunately, Mr. Cooke became aware of the short lived problem at a time when he was looking for something to get upset about. He quickly seized the opportunity and started ranting at me, telling me I was ultimately responsible for the performance of the house staff; that I should be supervising their every move and things should always be done ONLY ONE WAY: HIS WAY.

I tried to justify my actions concerning the houseman, who had recently immigrated to the U.S., and then I made the BIG mistake of standing up for him. Then I dug my hole even deeper. I told Mr. Cooke I respected immigrants because they had the courage to leave their native countries and move to the U.S. to make better lives for themselves and their families. Mr. Cooke couldn't believe his ears. He was shocked speechless by my comment. He looked at me without saying a word for several seconds and then exclaimed at the top of his voice "WHY DO YOU THINK THEY ARE SERVANTS? THEY'RE STUPID AND WILL NEVER BE ANYTHING ELSE AND THEREFORE MUST BE TREATED AS SUCH!"

Oh my god, I thought, the things that come out of this man's mouth! Can it get any worse? I was truly shocked by what he had said and prayed he wouldn't say anything else and that he'd turn around and walk out of my office and leave me alone. I couldn't bear to hear another word out of him. Thankfully, he went out for a long lunch and didn't bother me for the rest of the day. Quitting time didn't come fast enough. As I drove home, my mind was still reeling at the evil words Mr. Cooke had spewed earlier that day. I had to remind myself over and over again that, no matter what obstacles he tossed in my way, I needed to toughen up, keep moving forward and never forget my two-year goal, much like a climber on his way to the summit of Mount Everest. This recitation became my mantra.

CHAPTER 11

Where is the houseman?

On January 2 at about 12:30 in the afternoon, I was working in my office when Mr. Cooke called me from his bedroom. He was very frustrated and asked me where the houseman was, that he and Mrs. Cooke needed dishes cleared from the bedroom. I explained that the houseman was on his break and would be back shortly. Big mistake! For the next several minutes I caught holy hell for allowing the houseman to take a break during lunchtime. I held the phone about a foot away from my ear, while on and on he went, and only brought it to my mouth for the many times I had to repeat the required "yes sir". I had finally learned that if I just let him rant and give him his "yes sir" responses, the verbal onslaught would eventually end and things would return to normal – if there was such a thing.

This was the first of many times this houseman would get me into hot water with Mr. Cooke. He was the kind of guy who got everyone in trouble and I had quickly learned I couldn't trust him and had to watch him every single minute. I was also learning to not be so naive and trusting and to question everything the houseman or any of the other house staff did.

CHAPTER 12

"I could kill you"

On January 7 at about 12:10 pm, Mr. Cooke had not yet emerged for the day. His general counsel was on the phone and, despite my reluctance to do so, he insisted I ring him through to Mr. Cooke. He told me it was urgent. Though my gut was screaming at me not to do it, I put the call through to Mr. Cooke's bedroom. After all, having only been there for six weeks, who was I to second guess Mr. Cooke's counsel, especially when I had learned the day before that the matter really was important.

Things stayed quiet for the next 30 minutes so I figured everything was ok. Suddenly, out of nowhere, Mr. Cooke appeared in my office and, with hands on his hips, he angrily glared down at me and growled in his low, abrasive Trevor Howard-like voice "I could kill you". My blood ran ice cold and I thought I would shit my pants. No one had ever spoken to me like that and I didn't know what to do! He was really angry. He said I should have told his counsel he wasn't there.

Damned if you do and damned if you don't!!! I sat there dumbfounded. I couldn't seem to get anything right! Over the years, I had always been able to use my good judgment, follow my gut, and anticipate whatever my boss might need. But with this guy, there was no clear cut way. The Jack Kent Cooke way was one obtuse detour after another until you were hopelessly lost. True North was non- existent in the land of Cooke. The only thing you could do was hang on to the big horse and let it run.

Later that same day, I was working in my office when again, out of nowhere, Mr. Cooke suddenly appeared at my desk, again with his hands on his hips, again glaring down at me. And again he growled the same menacing threat, "I could kill you". Apparently, without knowing I should have had a letter he had written to his young daughter (whose mother the staff was required to refer to as "The Bitch") in Middleburg delivered by hand, I had committed the unforgiveable sin of mailing it. Call out the firing squad! She's really done it this time!

After delivering his second death threat of the day, Mr. Cooke returned to the library. I couldn't believe this had happened twice in the same day! I thought to myself, "why don't you just go ahead and kill me then. Put me out of my misery because I can't stand working for you another minute". Maybe it would be acceptable on my resume if the reason for leaving was my own death? I wondered who else in the world would tolerate this excessive amount of crap? Was I crazy to stay? Or was I doing the right thing by sticking it out for two years? It took me several minutes to recover from the threats. My entire body was trembling and I couldn't think straight.

Mr. Cooke continued to treat me like a criminal of the worst kind until it was almost time for me to go home. It took everything I had to keep from not quitting and walking out. As soon as I could break away for a few minutes, I went for a quick walk to a nearby store and bought a paper to look at the job ads, even though I knew I probably wouldn't do anything. It was a small independent action on my part just to remind myself that I was still a free agent and could leave whenever I wanted. This would be the first of many walks like this that I would take from Marbella while working for Mr. Cooke.

Somehow he seemed to know I needed to go for that walk. When it was time for me to go home, and after he had had a glass of wine, he was back to calling me a "wonderful darling and a pet". Ugh! I wanted to throw up! I wondered if he was insane or if he was going to make me insane. I jumped in my car, drove straight home and grabbed my workout clothes, then drove straight to the health club and attacked the Stairmaster.

I was so angry and upset, I couldn't sleep that night. In my mind, I argued with Mr. Cooke all night long. I returned to work the next morning, my stomach in knots and the tension building as I got closer to Marbella. I didn't want to go in there! I felt like Daniel walking into the lion's den. I entered the house through the kitchen, removed my shoes, put on my slippers, and tip toed into my office. The house was very quiet; Mr. Cooke was still sleeping. I was still upset from the day before and wondered what sort of horrific behavior I was in for today.

I felt cheated that I was rendered mute, unable to speak up and defend my actions, but any sort of confrontation with Mr. Cooke was out of the question and would never be tolerated. I had found that there was one way in which Mr. Cooke would accept any kind of input from his lowly serfs and that was by written communication. That worked fine for me because I was much better at writing. I sat down and wrote what would be the first of many letters to Mr. Cooke.

Dear Mr. Cooke,

During the past 6 1/2 weeks I have found myself saying "I am sorry" more than I have during my whole lifetime. I don't seem to be able to do anything right for you. This concerns me a great deal, because I know I am an intelligent, competent, responsible and professional executive assistant. I have always prided myself for my first-rate judgment and instincts. Most unfortunately, you seem to be convinced otherwise.

I completely understand what I am to do now if anyone other than (X) or (X) calls and says the matter is urgent. However, I must justify my actions to you: only having been in your employ for 6 weeks, and lacking specific instructions for when people call you before you have emerged for the day,

I felt it was not up to me to question the judgment of one of your executive staff. When your general counsel called at 12:10 pm on Tuesday and insisted on being put through, I put him through only after confirming with him more than once that it was indeed urgent.

No one, especially me, enjoys getting yelled at or reprimanded for something they do not know about. If I specifically did something wrong or neglected to do something I was told to do, I would expect my employer to be annoyed. But I find myself constantly apprehensive of being reprimanded by you throughout the day. And that is not a good feeling.

You have said over and over again that I am too nice a person. I think you like me because of that. You might also say that I am too sensitive, that I should not take your reprimands personally. Yes, I will admit I am sensitive. But it is still better to be sensitive rather than unfeeling or apathetic.

Please tell me what I can do for you, Mr. Cooke, that will please you and keep you reasonably happy. Please inform me of any other procedures which I know nothing about so that I will be able to perform them. I take great pride in doing my job and keeping my boss happy.

I want to feel good about coming to Marbella to work each day. I want to do a good job for you. I sincerely hope you will take my concerns to heart, Mr. Cooke.

Sincerely

I folded the letter and put it in an envelope and addressed it to "Mr. Cooke" and set it right in the middle of his desk so he couldn't miss it. I returned to my office and waited, my heart pounding in my chest. A short while later Mr. Cooke came into the library, sat down at his desk, read my letter, and asked me to come into the library. He dissected my letter with the enthusiasm of a medical examiner performing his first autopsy on a murder victim that had just arrived at the morgue. He discussed every sentence from beginning to end and focused on my proper (improper, according to Mr. Cooke) use of the English language. By the time "our" one-sided discussion was over, I wasn't sure if it had gone well or not. It had seemed more like an English logic class I had taken in college, the real reason for the letter swept aside and forgotten. Nevertheless, I hoped what I had said in the letter would keep Mr. Cooke on the passive side, at least for the time being.

CHAPTER 13

A little trip to the Super Bowl

The Redskins were going to the Super Bowl! The Kent Farms staff and I had just two short weeks to plan Mr. Cooke's Super Bowl trip. It was to be a three-day party for him and over 100 of his closest friends. We needed to charter a Boeing 747, telephone each person on the list and personally extend Mr. Cooke's invitation, reserve guest rooms for everyone and make sure all of their special needs were taken care of, and plan all of the special events leading up to the big game which Mr. Cooke would host.

It was a massive undertaking and one of the few times I would team up with the two secretaries from Kent Farms. It felt very odd to address them as Mrs. (X) instead of by their first names, but that wasn't allowed and I wasn't going to risk another tongue lashing a la Cooke. I was glad to be busy with such a big project. My days were full and my work had a steady pace and rhythm, like a sailboat slicing through the water, its sails filled with wind. Everything felt right; I was on a steady course for once, moving swiftly and confidently, and I felt less of a target for Mr. Cooke's frequent attacks. Eventually, all of the invitations had been extended and RSVPs received, all the arrangements made, and all the logistics taken care of. All we had to do now was wait for the big show.

Two days before the Super Bowl, the chartered 747 took off from Dulles Airport for Minneapolis. After the endless hours of frenzied activity ensuring that Mr. Cooke's three days of entertaining all his guests and fulfilling his responsibilities as NFL owner went off without a hitch, I stayed behind in DC (not that I ever had a choice), thankful for the peace and quiet. I would depend on the local TV stations to give me updates on the events in Minneapolis. The only thing I cared about was that Mr. Cooke was out of my hair for a few days and I would get a much needed break.

CHAPTER 14

Caressing the Super Bowl trophy

The day that every football fan dreams about had finally arrived and, as expected, the Redskins dominated Buffalo and emerged victorious at Super Bowl XXVI. I watched the game with friends at a party and, I must admit, enjoyed all the attention I received because of my connection with the team. It was fun to see Mr. Cooke celebrate with his winning team on TV. He was king of the world and he knew it. He was all smiles as he shook hands with everyone and accepted congratulatory hugs. I especially loved seeing him and Coach Gibbs hug each other and share the excitement.

It wasn't long, though, before all my fun was quickly overshadowed by the sobering realization that Mr. Cooke was due back home the next day. My few short days of peace and quiet had come to an end!

When Mr. Cooke's limo pulled into Marbella, I greeted him at the door with a congratulatory kiss and hug. I saw right away that he was exhausted. After all, he was almost 80 years old and he had been traveling and entertaining non-stop for three days, a tall order for anyone. I stood at the door while the house staff brought in all the luggage from the limo. Suddenly, someone thrust a big silver thing into my arms and said "here, take this". I couldn't believe it when I realized it was the Super Bowl trophy!

The Super Bowl trip had taken its toll. Mr. Cooke was very irritable and just plain worn out. And to add fuel to the fire, his son, Ralph, who managed Mr. Cooke's race horse farm in Kentucky, Elmendorf, had promised he'd come to Marbella for dinner that night but it was going on 5 o'clock and no one had heard from him. Thinking that Ralph had left town without saying good bye, Mr. Cooke was upset and in a dangerous mood. I nervously watched as he looked for any excuse to take his foul mood out on some poor unfortunate soul. Needless to say, the rest of the staff and I were very relieved when Ralph finally showed up and Mr. Cooke was happy again.

All things considered, it had been a good day at Marbella. I had seen my boss return home a Super Bowl champion and I had even held the Super Bowl trophy. I wondered how many other people could say that?

CHAPTER 15

Bloody Wednesday

Two days after his triumphant return from the Super Bowl, Mr. Cooke was still worn out from the trip and stayed in bed. He was irritable beyond belief, like a small child who had been denied his afternoon nap. Early in the day, Mrs. Cooke's older son was going to the post office and offered to take my mail. It seemed a natural thing and couldn't possibly cause a problem, so I thanked him and handed him the mail and off he went. Uh oh. Mr. Cooke saw what I had done and suddenly got angry, telling me NOT to do his thinking for him, that the houseman (who normally took the mail every day at 5 o'clock) would NOT deviate from the usual schedule.

Oh my God, I thought, doesn't he have anything better to do with his time than worry about who takes the mail to the post office? He never failed to amaze me from day to day with all the little things he could find to explode over. It made no sense to me. He was a billionaire for God's sake. He could afford to hire professionally trained housemen and butlers and cooks – anything he wanted — but instead, he hired his help off the street. I could only assume he did that just so he could have people around that he could bully. He didn't know how to do it any other way.

About an hour before quitting time, Mr. Cooke called me into his bedroom where he was in bed, reading. I knocked gently on the door and went in and stood alongside his bed. He quietly looked at me for a couple of seconds and then he chewed me out non-stop for a solid 20 minutes for LETTING THE HOUSE GO TO HELL today. I stood there, helpless, my hands down at my sides and my insides turning to ice, responding "yes sir" and "I'm sorry sir" over and over again. Saying anything else would have been unacceptable. On and on he went, telling me I had allowed the servants to take breaks (their first breaks in several days!) and that I should never have done so. He threatened to fire me and then said I should stop thinking of myself for a change (What? Where was all of this coming from?), that even the housekeeper worked harder than me. He shook his head, told me he didn't know what to do with me and dismissed me, telling me to go back to work.

Just like that I was back in hell again. How much more of this could I take? Again, I remembered my two-year commitment to myself and pushed the negative thoughts out of my mind.

From then on, I needed to be very careful and plan ahead and figure out what could possibly go wrong because sure as hell it would go wrong. Murphy's Law ruled in that house like none other!

CHAPTER 16

The house that Jack built

After the Redskins' Super Bowl victory and once he recovered from his trip, Mr. Cooke's energy level knew no limits. It was the right time to move ahead with his plans for the new Jack Kent Cooke Stadium, the new home for his Super Bowl champions. Marbella quickly became a hub for meetings with stadium architects, banking executives and local politicians whose jurisdictions were being considered for the home of the stadium.

Mr. Cooke threw himself completely into the project. After all, it would become his swan song, his legacy, the house that Jack built. It was a huge project and would require the approval of the state of Virginia or the District of Columbia or the state of Maryland, as well as local districts. Construction loans had to be arranged and there would be endless permit application processes. And, of course, there was major speculation and opinion amongst the public as to exactly where the stadium would and should end up. Virginia, Maryland or the District of Columbia?

CHAPTER 17

Poached eggs anyone?

All was quiet. I was working in my office and Mr. Cooke hadn't yet emerged from his bedroom. Suddenly, the cook appeared in my office and told me that Mr. Cooke wanted poached eggs PREPARED IN A PROPER EGG POACHER for his breakfast. There was just one problem: there was no "proper" egg poacher in the house. I asked the cook if he could just poach the eggs in water but he just shook his head because he knew that would be unacceptable.

I knew exactly what Mr. Cooke wanted because I had one at home, an old fashioned shallow aluminum pan with a frame in it that held removable aluminum cups for the eggs. It operated like a double boiler, the boiling water just touching the bottoms of the cups and the steam circulating within the covered pot would poach the eggs. Unfortunately, I hadn't seen a poacher like that in the stores for years. I knew we had our work cut out for us because the words "can't" and "no" weren't acceptable to Mr. Cooke.

"Mission Impossible" quickly fell on my shoulders when Mr. Cooke told me to go out and find a poacher. I went to Sears and they had none. I went to every other place I could think of within a reasonable distance but there was no egg poacher to be found. I ran out of options.

If you really thought about it, it was actually comical. The entire Cooke household had gone into crisis mode because the king required a proper egg poacher. Here I was in total panic mode desperately searching all over the District of Columbia and surrounding area for a poacher. I was sure the cook was standing in the kitchen watching the clock, perspiration dripping down his face. And I was absolutely positive Mr. Cooke was pacing back and forth between the kitchen and his bedroom, repeating over and over again "Where is she? Good God all I asked for was an egg poacher!"

I returned poacherless. I had failed my mission. In an attempt to ease his temper, I told Mr. Cooke I'd look for one during the coming weekend and, if I still couldn't find one, I'd give him mine, to which he imperiously replied "YOU WILL DO NOTHING OF THE SORT! SUPPOSE I WANT POACHED EGGS TOMORROW MORNING?" I laughed to myself. I should have known better. It seemed like every time I tried to be nice to him or offer a solution, it only made things worse and his response always ended up hurting my feelings. When would I learn?

The next day, two "proper" egg poachers miraculously arrived from Kent Farms and Mr. Cooke had his poached eggs.

Now that he had thrown his tantrum and had had his poached eggs, Mr. Cooke was as nice as he could be. He even told me he was sorry for his behavior and remarked that he "should have been placed in a sanatorium". I thought yeah, no kidding, and offered no response. He continued to be jocular and playful and then, at mid-day, told me he was "done in" and "not well at all" and disappeared into his bedroom for the remainder of the day.

CHAPTER 18

Dear Mr. Cooke (again)

In the last three months, I had been chewed out more than I had in my entire life. Mr. Cooke had said awful things to me. He had been rude and hurtful and I was fed up. After long, hard thought, I gave up on the two-year promise I made to myself and typed up a memo telling Mr. Cooke I was leaving. I was waiting until the time was right to give it to him. I thought the next time he gets nasty and pushes me into a corner, I'm gonna come out swinging.

I didn't have to wait long. Again he was upset with me … I was a great disappointment to him … he didn't know what he was going to do with me … we were not going to get along, et cetera, et cetera, et cetera. So I just looked up at him and said "You're right, Mr. Cooke, we have a problem and we are not going to get along, so I have decided to look elsewhere for employment."

Hmm, ball in Mr. Cooke's court. He leaned back in his chair for a minute and processed what I had said. He then said he completely agreed with me, that he would start looking for a replacement and I should start looking for another job right away. He called the manager at Kent Farms and told her to start looking for my replacement. He told me he'd give me a reference and wished me luck.

The bully had won. He had beat me down and he was pleased with his victory. I hoped he was satisfied. The former mayor of DC had pegged him perfectly when she publicly proclaimed him a "Billionaire Bully". I laughed bitterly to myself.

Before I left that evening, I placed the resignation letter I had been saving on his desk. I wasn't going to leave without telling him exactly what I thought. After all, I now had nothing to lose.

Dear Mr. Cooke,

After several of our recent "talks" it appears obvious to me that you are never going to be satisfied with my performance. Therefore, in order to save us both a lot of stress and tension, I plan to look for employment elsewhere.

You said I should stop thinking of myself for a change, that the housekeeper works harder than me. Mr. Cooke, I have not taken any lunch breaks since I came to work for you simply because I wanted to be available whenever you needed me, whether you were here at Marbella or away. Furthermore, outside of being tied up in a bad traffic situation beyond my control which caused me to be 5 minutes late for work one morning, I have been at work at least 20 minutes early every morning. I have stayed late on several occasions. I have, without question, adjusted my work hours whenever you have asked. I have tried to stay on top of the situation with the houseman to keep Marbella the way you want it kept.

You said maybe you should treat me like this (referring to your reprimand of Wed Jan 29) every day so I'll just want to leave. I don't know what else to do for you. I am very sorry it has not worked out between us. But I simply cannot stomach the severe tongue lashings you so frequently administer. And so, along the lines of your foregoing reasoning, I have chosen to leave. Not because I am incapable of doing the job, but because of your consistent lack of satisfaction with my performance as evidenced in your recent remarks.

I, too, am extremely disappointed with this situation. The last thing I want to do is return to what is presently a very challenging job market. But I feel it will be best for you and me in the long run as my "lack of performance", as you see it, seems to be the cause of much of your stress and, therefore, mine.

You are indeed a remarkable man, Mr. Cooke, and I have appreciated the opportunity to work for you.

Best
Catherine Crozier

When I showed up at work the next morning, Mr. Cooke asked me to come into the library, where I sat in the chair at his desk opposite him. He said he was very touched by my letter. He said we were going to get along very well after all, that he would be crazy to let me go, and try to replace someone as good as me, and would I please reconsider and stay. I was shocked! I realized that this was just a game for Mr. Cooke and he had been testing me. Ha! Almost 80 years old, wealthy beyond anyone's dreams, king of his empire, and he still felt like he had to play his hurtful games and treat people badly. One would have thought, or at least hoped, that at this late stage of his life he would have learned some humility and to treat others with kindness and respect.

I looked Mr. Cooke square in the eye. I asked him if he would ease up on me. He smiled and said he would. Then I said "will you shake hands on that Mr. Cooke?" and he laughed and extended his hand and we shook.

He kept his promise for about five weeks.

CHAPTER 19

The romantic

It was Valentine's Day and romance was in the air, Cooke style. While Mrs. Cooke was out shopping (her favorite pastime), Mr. Cooke had a beautiful bouquet of roses delivered to Marbella. He practically rearranged his whole office to compose the perfect setting for the roses. He experimented with different backgrounds, lighting, etc and kept asking me what I thought, not that my opinion ever mattered.

Once he had everything arranged to his satisfaction, he waited impatiently, pacing back and forth in his office and walking in and out of my office, like an expectant father, waiting for his bride to come home. I was thankful it was time for me to leave before Mrs. Cooke showed up. Three was a crowd.

CHAPTER 20

Hangin' out with Alta

When things got really tough, it was time to head up to Maryland for an Alta fix. A weekend at Alta's could provide a cure for anything. It was always pure comic relief. Alta's middle name was "Weird". If anything was odd, strange, off beat or just plain bizarre, she not only knew about it, chances were she was involved in it. Whenever we were together, we made it our mission to find the whimsical, magical, cosmic stuff that, if you were lucky, life might share with you.

On Friday night, my sanity hanging on by a thread after a long week with Mr. Cooke, I packed a bag, grabbed Dickens and made the 70 mile drive to the farm in Maryland where Alta and her husband, Dave, and their young daughter, Katie, lived. Tension turned to relief as soon as I turned my car north, away from Cooke's domain. My life would be my own for two glorious days! I always looked forward to getting off of the highway and onto the small, quiet country roads that wound their way into the hilly and picturesque farmland where Alta lived.

As I approached one particular curvy, dippy section of the road, I slowed down and pulled a towel into my lap and put Dickens on top of it and then continued driving. Dickens was prone to motion sickness and tossed his cookies right in this spot every time. Soon came the pathetic meow, his way of warning me that I had about 10 seconds before the projectile vomiting would commence. Thank heavens for towels and good planning! The crisis soon over, I relaxed and began to eagerly anticipate my arrival at the farm.

The farm on the hilltop soon came into view and what a welcome sight it was. I turned off the road and started up the long curving driveway bordered on both sides by pastures with grazing sheep and the occasional lama. At the top of the hill, I passed by the "big house" where the owners lived, past the barn that was home to the sheep and lamas and Alta's horses, past a couple more pastures and, finally, pulled up to Alta's tiny cottage.

I had already begun to relax and knew my visit would be just what the doctor ordered. This was my safe place. This was where I would receive unconditional love, friendship and support, with no questions asked. This was where my buildup of protective armor would be gently and painlessly chizzled away until, at last, my vulnerable and fun self would come alive again. I knew there would be great food ("hot, brown and plenty of it"), and I knew we would laugh until we almost peed our pants. And, for the icing on the cake, I also knew chances were good that something really weird and funny would happen, because this was the place where the unexpected was expected.

As I gathered up Dickens and my bag, Alta came outside, her arms stretched out for a big hug, accompanied by her trademark "heeeeyyyyyyy" in that low voice of hers. I took in a big breath of the fresh air and listened to the blessed peace and quiet of the countryside. Dickens, an indoor cat, always loved going to Alta's too. I couldn't imagine how excited his senses must have got when he went from the everyday tedium of our small apartment to what must have surely seemed like the circus to him. For a cat, it was a smorgasbord of smells and animals! Alta shared her tiny home with parakeets, a bunny, two large collies, and anything else that had feathers or fur that showed up and needed a little help. And that was more than enough to keep Mr. Dickens occupied. After his first few visits, he had the two collies completely bullied and it was not unusual to see both of them cowered into a corner by a triumphant looking Dickens just sitting there innocently looking at them.

Alta had prepared a superb dinner: roast stuffed chicken, mashed potatoes, gravy and string beans. My favorite comfort food. Now, the reader should be forewarned here about table manners in the Reynolds household. There were none. It was every man / woman / child for him or herself, and the family motto was "more for me". One learned very quickly not to get between a Reynolds armed with a fork and any food on the table that was fair game. Within minutes the delicious meal was devoured. The few leftover scraps were fed to the dogs and the dishes washed. Our bellies full, Alta and I sat back down at the kitchen table with mugs of freshly brewed coffee and smoked our after dinner cigarettes. I could feel my armor starting to release its tenuous hold on me. My therapy had begun.

After our caffeine and nicotine fix, we went out to the barn to check on the horses and feed them. Then we just sat down on a couple of bales of hay and watched the horses and listened to their comforting familiar sounds. I told Alta all about the week I had had. My emotions were all over the place: from complete anger and frustration to disbelief to uncontrollable laughter at the sheer ludicrousness of it all. How did one describe life on Mars? I finished my report and we just sat there in the silence. I reached down and plucked a stem of sweet Timothy out of the hay bale and started chewing on it. At that moment, as if on cue, Alta's mare maneuvered her hind end in our direction, lifted her tail, and took a generous crap. I looked at Alta and she looked at me and, our heads tilted and eyebrows and shoulders raised, we both agreed that that about summed it all up. We laughed all the way back to the cottage. The armor was coming off fast.

Back in the house, we changed into sweats and PJs and plopped down in front of the TV with lots of pillows and hand stitched quilts. Watching TV at Alta's was always a special event. Whenever she knew I was coming up for a visit, she set her mind, as a hound dog sets its nose, to searching far and wide for the most extraordinary and bizarre movies. She found them in video stores and she found them (thanks to their giant C-band satellite dish) on TV channels that no one ever watched.

For that evening's viewing pleasure (Alta's words), we settled on *"Mystery Science Theater 3000"*. The format for this series was to show really bad, cornball black and white movies from the 1950s to robots from the future that were forced to watch them as some sort of punishment. You see the movie playing out on a movie theater screen and the silhouettes of the robots sitting in their front row seats. At the same time, you hear the robots feeding in their own funny lines and making jokes and comments about the cheesy dialogue in the movie. It was just way too funny and we laughed so hard we thought we were going to die. Needless to say, we became instant fans of "MST".

The next day, we were in the barn with three-year-old Katie, cleaning stalls, grooming horses and taking care of the other usual barn stuff. There were a few young roosters in the barn – the product of the farm owner's recent attempt at egg production – and one of them kept going after Katie, who was growing more terrified by the moment. Trying not to use too much force, Alta was able to keep the offending rooster at bay. That is, until the one moment when no one was looking and the persistent rooster finally had his chance to make contact with Katie.

Hearing Katie's scream, Alta was on the rooster at lightning speed and, as if in slow motion, her foot connected with the rooster's hind end and, in the perfect form of the Redskins' kicker, Alta sent the shocked rooster sailing straight up into the air and right over the barn rafter. Just before Alta launched the offending rooster, Dave arrived in the barn and witnessed the perfect 3 pointer. We all looked at him and, with perfect comedic timing, he silently signaled a successful field goal by raising his arms straight up. Oh my god it was so funny! We all laughed so hard we were dying. This was the kind of stuff we lived for! The magic had happened. And most important, I was my old self again. That little episode would keep us in stitches for years and become one of our favorite stories.

On Sunday, we said our goodbyes and, reinvigorated and refortified, I returned home, ready to face Mr. Cooke again.

CHAPTER 21

Louder. . . I can't hear you!

About a week after Valentine's Day, it was about an hour before the Cookes' dinner time, and Mr. & Mrs. Cooke were enjoying wine and hors d'oeuvres and quiet conversation in the library. I was working in my office and the door that connected my office to the library was wide open. Mrs. Cooke's older son, a quiet, seemingly shy 19 year old boy of slight build and unremarkable appearance, innocently came into the room to visit with them. After a few minutes of the usual pleasantries, Mr. Cooke suddenly and without warning, started yelling at him, shouting that he was stupid and unintelligent and uneducated. And as if that wasn't enough, he told the boy that even his friends had said the same things about him, which I was surprised to hear because there was no way I could imagine Mr. Cooke spending time with any of the boy's friends.

Not yet satisfied, Mr. Cooke shoved into the stunned boy's hands a letter that had been sitting on his desk and ordered him to read it out loud. Terrified, the boy held the letter in his shaking hands and, as he slowly read in a barely audible voice, Mr. Cooke interrupted him over and over again, shouting "LOUDER - - I CAN'T HEAR YOU" in that trademark bullying voice of his.

I was mortified! I couldn't believe what I was witnessing! I desperately wanted to close my door but I couldn't move for fear of calling attention to myself. I tried to make myself as small as I could and wished I could just disappear. I wondered for the umpteenth time how in the world Mr. Cooke could treat someone so horribly. Every day, it seemed his attacks on the boy grew worse and, if possible, even more obnoxious.

That was so painful to watch and my heart ached for Mrs. Cooke's son. I felt terrible for him. It wasn't his fault that his mother had never paid much attention to his education. And what was even more shocking to me was the fact that all during the attack, she just sat there and never said a single word in defense of her son.

CHAPTER 22

Stay out of the kitchen!

After armies of staff had scrambled for days to make all the detailed plans and arrangements for Mr. & Mrs. Cooke and the two boys to travel to the Bahamas in Mr. Cooke's private jet and charter a luxurious yacht, they had finally left town. Hooray! Everyone could finally catch their breath and have a well deserved break after all the frenzy of the past several days. Unfortunately, the Cookes had only been away for a few days when Mr. Cooke became restless and started calling every few hours. I didn't think he had any idea how to completely get away and relax.

On the day he began calling, I had a sore throat and went to the kitchen to get a glass of ice water. The moment I stepped into the kitchen, Mr. Cooke called. I guess he could tell I wasn't in my office because he asked me where I was. I told him I was in the kitchen. Well, I might as well have told him I was in the game room goofing off and helping myself to his Chateau Margeaux. He was very upset that I was "AWAY FROM THE POST OF COMMAND"! He told me I was going to "LOSE THE RESPECT OF THE SERVANTS AND MY AUTHORITY WOULD BE REDUCED IF I SPENT TOO MUCH TIME IN THE KITCHEN BECOMING TOO FAMILIAR WITH THE SERVANTS". After the shock of his outburst wore off, I tried to explain that I was getting a glass of ice water and he angrily cut me off and yelled "YOU CAN GET A GLASS OF WATER IN YOUR BATHROOM, WOMAN! STAY OUT OF THE KITCHEN!". "Oh you are such a nasty cranky man!" I shouted to myself. I uttered the obligatory "yes sir" and he said good bye and hung up.

I was completely humiliated and returned to my office which I had now come to think of as my prison cell. I could look out on the gardens and pool through the French doors but I couldn't go out and enjoy them even for a few minutes for fear Mr. Cooke would call. I was even afraid to go to the bathroom.

I stayed out of the kitchen for the next day and a half. I was scared to death to even think about going in there, even though I needed to drink more water than usual because of my sore throat, but I didn't want to keep bothering the cook. When I finally did get my nerve up to make the forbidden trip to the kitchen, the moment my foot stepped onto the kitchen floor, the phone rang and I just knew it was Mr. Cooke! Somehow he knew I was back in there! In a total panic, I yelled to the cook to answer the phone and, so I would have time to run back to my office, tell Mr. Cooke I was I the bathroom even though I knew that would piss him off too. Then, as fast as I could, I ran back to my office, trying not to slip on the marble floor in my socks! I wondered who in the world would believe this nonsense actually happened!

CHAPTER 23

Help! I'm trapped in a $3 million home and the servants are feeding me to death!

While the Cookes were on vacation, the house staff was much more relaxed and enjoying a more normal atmosphere and pace. I think they decided they liked me and they certainly proved it that week.

The new houseman needed to learn how to properly serve dinner to the Cookes, so, the cook asked me to stay after work each night that week and have dinner there so the houseman could practice serving. Each night, shoeless, I sat at one of the two small round dining tables that were set in the far end of the huge, cold, marble floored living room. I was served formally by the houseman and ate and drank from Mr. Cooke's priceless fine china and crystal. This was my first and only time experiencing this style of dining reserved for the ultra wealthy and privileged. To tell the truth, I would much rather have been at home in my sweats with my feet up in front of the TV, my dinner in my lap and Dickens at my side.

Toward the end of the week while the Cookes were still away, the gastronomic delights continued. Late one afternoon, continuing his training, the houseman showed up in my office bearing a silver tray of hors d'oeuvres the cook had prepared for me. Also, the cook surprised me several times with wonderful lunches. Even the housekeeper got into the act and made a noontime appearance in my office, delivering the results of her cooking efforts of the day: Spanish style steak, broccoli and rice.

I never thought I would say it but I would be thankful when Mr. Cooke returned so I could get back to my regular eating routine. Someone please give this poor girl a hot dog or tuna fish sandwich!

CHAPTER 24

You are my secretary, not my dog handler!

Apparently the Cookes were having trouble in paradise. Mrs. Cooke did not return to Marbella with Mr. Cooke after they came back from their vacation and she was still gone. I learned from the house staff that she told Mr. Cooke she wanted a divorce. Knowing him pretty well by now I braced myself for the worst. Now he really did have a good reason to be upset and in a foul mood. All things considered though, he was doing pretty well. At least until yesterday, when he never got dressed or showered or shaved. He had just walked around in his silk dressing robe all day and was uncharacteristically quiet. I actually felt bad for him, even after all the crap he had put me through; though secretly, I wanted to ask him "so, Mr. Cooke, how does it feel to be humiliated?".

The next day when I arrived for work and walked into the library, I was greeted by the comical sight of Mr. Cooke, the houseman and the cook, all on their knees in the library. Oh how I loved seeing men down on their knees. I thought, "what on earth is going on here?". The cook told me they were looking for Mr. Cooke's hearing aid which had popped out of his ear. I quickly joined them, laughing to myself. What a sight we were, all four of us crawling around on our knees. Eventually the AWOL hearing aid was found and another crisis was averted. After receiving a hasty thank you and dismissal from Mr. Cooke, everyone returned to their battle stations.

Mr. Cooke remained in his robe, unshowered and unshaved, until about noon. I was relieved when he finally disappeared into his bedroom to get cleaned up and dressed. He was still quiet and contemplative, though, and was starting to remind me of a smoldering pile of garbage about to erupt into spontaneous combustion. I sat in my office and waited for the explosion.

Later in the afternoon, as I sat opposite Mr. Cooke at his desk, Mrs. Cooke's poodle "Chanel" walked up to my chair and hopped onto my lap. She settled right down and lay there very quietly with her head across my left arm and I gently stroked her. The poor little thing was obviously missing Mrs. Cooke. After a couple of minutes, Mr. Cooke asked me not to do that and barked "You are my secretary, not my dog handler". Yikes! I immediately removed the startled dog from my lap and didn't say a word.

The estranged Mrs. Cooke returned to Marbella a couple of days later. Mr. Cooke was like a nervous stallion in a paddock next to a bunch of hot mares. He was determined to put on a show for her. He was looking at everything, suspicious of everything, questioning everything, doing everything he could to impress her. He buzzed me into his office every 20 seconds. I might as well have just stood there in front of them and done an Irish jig. Oh well, at least he wasn't screaming or yelling at me which was a huge relief.

Shortly after Mrs. Cooke returned to Marbella, I ran into her on my way into work one morning. Up until then, I had only seen her completely made up and dressed to the nines. This time though, she had no makeup on and was in sweats. I couldn't believe how hard and common she looked. Wow, I thought, anything can be accomplished when you've got a limitless supply of money.

CHAPTER 25

Hangin' with Alta: lambing season

It was time for another run up to Alta's. It was lambing season and that was always fun. Dickens and I pulled up to Alta's cottage just before lunchtime on Saturday. An exhausted Alta dragged herself out to the car to greet us. I took one look at her and said "Oh my God you look like shit!" She laughed and then enlightened me on the quality of life of a shepherd during lambing season. For the past week, once lambing had started, she had to check on the pregnant ewes every hour, including during the night, because they always needed help with lambing and there were things that needed to be done right away for the baby lambs. It was very labor intensive. On the weekends, the owner of the farm took the night shift so Alta could catch up on rest. That was fine with me because I needed some R&R myself. Dave was away on a business trip, so we planned a low-key weekend for just us girls: good food, good movies and good old hangin' out. A nice little hen party. Dress code: sweats. It didn't get much better than that.

We had some lunch and, while little Katie entertained herself with Dickens and the collies, Alta and I got caught up on everything. It was cold and wet outside and it seemed like a good day to wrap ourselves in the quilts and watch movies or work on our current cross stitch projects. Later that afternoon I cooked dinner so Alta could rest. I had brought along everything I needed to make my sister Patty's award-winning Minestrone. It was the perfect thing for a cold rainy day. After an hour of peeling, chopping and sauteeing, a pot of Minestrone was finally simmering on the stove.

At around 5 o'clock we walked to the barn to check on the horses and feed them. They had been kept inside all day because of the weather and welcomed us with soft nickers. I lifted Katie up so she could help put hay into each of the stalls. After we refilled the water buckets and made sure everyone was ok, we decided to look in on the ewes. Lo and behold one of them was doing her thing! Alta got right into shepherd mode and dived right in. The next thing I knew she was running to a large empty stall, carrying a very still and quiet newborn lamb, still partially covered in birth membrane. She stepped to the middle of the stall and, holding the lifeless lamb by its hind feet, she turned herself into a human centrifuge, spinning the lamb for about 30 seconds. She then set the lamb down into the straw and just like that the lamb starting breathing and making its precious little "baa" noises. Alta gently picked up the minutes-old lamb and carried it to its mother who commenced to licking her baby clean, all the while making her motherly grunts to her baby. I was humbled and awestruck. I had never seen anything like that before and was incredibly impressed by the cool and calm demeanor with which Alta had handled the tense situation. Her previous experience as assistant to a large animal veterinarian had definitely paid off.

After the farm owner arrived and took over, Alta, Katie and I scurried back to the house, shielding ourselves from the driving rain. I was still speechless from what I had witnessed. When we stepped into the warm, cozy cottage, we were instantly overwhelmed by the heavenly smells coming from the kitchen. The Minestrone was ready! We cleaned up and got into warm, dry clothes. I set the table and once Alta and Katie were seated I served them steaming bowls of the delicious, hearty soup. We each had seconds, Katie included. The Minestrone was always a big crowd pleaser.

After we cleaned up the kitchen, fed all the critters and had our coffee and after dinner cigarettes, we moved into the TV room to watch a movie. Tonight's choice was *The Big Lebowski* – another one of Alta's recent discoveries. The Coen Brothers movie starred Jeff Bridges, John Goodman and Steve Buscemi and was about a pacifist, "The Dude" (played by Bridges), who is the victim of a case of mistaken identity at the hands of some henchmen who end up attacking him and peeing on his single prized possession, an oriental rug. All The Dude wanted was to have his rug replaced by the right guy, the older, fabulously wealthy Big Lebowski. As one can imagine, this led to all kinds of chaos, strange circumstances and best of all, lots of great, ironic humor. The movie had a huge cult following and it was the ultimate crowning achievement of Alta's movie selection career. We became instant groupies of The Dude. We laughed till we cried. It was wonderful. It was so wonderful, in fact, that we would watch this movie over and over again and still do to this day.

We woke up Sunday to a beautiful sunny spring day. While we were on our second cup of coffee, Alta decided she wanted to take some pictures of Katie with the lambs. Maybe something with an Easter theme. So out came all of Katie's clothes and Alta's sewing supplies. Alta could do anything with a sewing machine; she was one of the most resourceful people I knew. Before I knew it, Katie was transformed into Little Bo Peep – bonnet and all. Alta grabbed her camera and out to the barn we went. The end result was a series of precious pictures of Little Bo Peep Katie surrounded by baby lambs.

After a quick lunch and an exchange of goodbye hugs, I left the tranquil and (somewhat) normal and sane rhythm of life on the farm on the hilltop and returned to my strange and fragile existence on the frontline of Mr. Cooke's world.

CHAPTER 26

Curmudgeon (again)

Mr. Cooke and I were working together at his desk, catching up on fan mail and correspondence, when he decided to call his son, John, who was Executive Director of the Redskins. He dialed a wrong number and, instead of hearing the expected "good morning, Redskins Park", he was surprised by a strange voice from, of all things, a cement company. Not sure what had happened, he asked for "Mr. John" (all corporate and Redskins front office staff were required to call him "Mr. John" because there was only one Mr. Cooke). When the lady who answered the phone asked Mr. Cooke what department "Mr. John" worked in, he then realized his mistake. Right then and there, in a split second, his stern, unfriendly face softened before my eyes and, with that mischievous smile and his light blue eyes glowing with curmudgeonliness, replied "I think he's in the sanitation department, you know, garbage removal". Oh this was priceless. The flustered woman then said "this is a concrete company" to which Mr. Cooke responded "well then, I think he's down there with the cement mixers". The poor woman was speechless, she didn't know what to say and you could tell she didn't want to be rude. Mr. Cooke finally laughed and, without identifying himself, told the woman he had called a wrong number and he was sorry to have bothered her and hung up. We both shared a good laugh over that, curmudgeon that he truly was. This little interlude had been unexpected and delightful. I had briefly glimpsed a man who could be completely disarming and irresistible. I wished he could be like that all the time.

Later that day, Mr. & Mrs. Cooke went to lunch at Duke's, his favorite place, where he had his own table and where he could hold court and be admired by his adoring public. I loved it when they went there because I knew he would always return in a great mood, especially after a couple of hours of special VIP treatment. This time, they were gone longer than usual and I began to wonder what was up. When they eventually returned to Marbella, it was obvious they were very much under the influence. Thank goodness he didn't try to do too much work! Mrs. Cooke went out shopping and Mr. Cooke quickly disappeared into his bedroom for a nap. As he made his exit from the library, he needlessly told me he would take no calls. Well. . . even the phone didn't dare ring for the rest of the afternoon.

CHAPTER 27

Good morning!! (like hell)

The last week had passed by without incident. I hadn't seen Mrs. Cooke but that wasn't unusual since she spent most of her time out shopping or visiting with friends away from Marbella. I kept hoping, for my sake, that she and Mr. Cooke would work things out and that life in the Kingdom of Cooke would be restored to a state that at least resembled something peaceful. Unfortunately, I didn't think that was going to happen because I had heard that Mrs. Cooke had recently been seen behaving, let's just say inappropriately, in a salsa bar in the Adams Morgan section of DC. Don't ask, don't tell.

Early yesterday, the houseman came to me and asked if he could have one of the Redskins shirts Mr. Cooke kept in my office, because the one he was wearing was soaked through with sweat. The first thing I did was tell him he needed to keep a supply of his own shirts at Marbella since he, to put it bluntly, sweat like a pig, and I couldn't keep on giving him Mr. Cooke's shirts. Against my better judgment, I gave him a shirt.

Mr. Cooke probably would never have found out about the shirt but that night, the houseman, not being the brightest person, interrupted Mr. & Mrs. Cooke's after dinner conversation in the library by walking right through the room, sans his required white houseman jacket, and into my office, where he took *another* shirt. He then went back through the library, *again* interrupting Mr. & Mrs. Cooke, and, in the process, even managed to yell "shut up" at Chanel when she barked at him. Ugh! Of course Mr. Cooke noticed the shirt in the houseman's hand and when he asked about it, the houseman told him I said he could have it.

So, the next morning, the second I entered the library on the way to my office, Mr. Cooke, who had been waiting for me, bellowed "HOW DARE YOU GIVE MY PROPERTY AWAY? WHATEVER POSSESSED YOU TO GIVE THE HOUSEMAN ONE OF MY SHIRTS YESTERDAY?" And on and on he went. He had told me I could take whatever shirts I needed, but I didn't dare remind him of that. He demanded that I pay for the shirt and said I should NEVER give away ANY of his "assets" no matter how small their value. I thought I would die on the spot, he made me feel so bad. He hadn't even said hello or good morning, he had just attacked and launched into the unnecessary and obnoxious reprimand. I wanted to explain to him why I had given the houseman the shirt but he gave me no opportunity. So, my insides turned to ice cubes, I had no choice but to stand there like a fool and let him go on until he exhausted himself and dismissed me.

Later on, while Mr. Cooke was out of the library, I left $8 on his desk for the shirt. When he found it, he brought it into my office and gave it back to me. He looked at me and said I was no good at supervising his servants and that I was to stop doing so immediately and only perform my secretarial duties for him. Yes! Thank you! That was fine with me! No one was ever going to be able to manage his house staff because it was impossible to keep him happy. What a relief!

I was still trying to recover from the ugly reprimand that morning and the temptation was growing stronger to just quit, to walk out and find another job and work with regular, normal people again. I had now worked for Mr. Cooke for five months and couldn't recall a single day that I had looked forward to coming to work. As a matter of fact, the closer I got to Marbella each morning, the sicker I felt. The stress was unbearable and I felt terrible. It even began to take a toll on my health. I talked to myself a lot those days and kept reminding myself over and over again how important it was to keep this job for at least two years.

CHAPTER 28

Didn't slavery end with the Civil War?

Today, I learned that Mr. Cooke told the houseman that this coming NFL season he'd be driving him to all the home games which were mostly on Sundays and, even though Sundays were his only day off, that he wouldn't be paid for those days. Then, unbelievably, Mr. Cooke told the houseman that he should make *him* pay for the privilege of driving him to the games!

That didn't surprise me at all. I knew Mr. Cooke well enough by now to know that he considered his "help" as chattel. In the land of Cooke, it was very simple: he owned them. He was the king and they were his serfs. He was the master and they were his slaves. They had no rights, none, zero. It was hard for me to watch. It made me think of Mel Brooks' movie *"The History of the World"* in which Brooks played King Louis XVI. While he was out strolling in the palace gardens, surrounded by members of his court, he would suddenly call out for the "piss boy", an unfortunate street urchin whose job was to follow the king with the royal piss bucket and hold it forth upon command. As King Louis XVI relieved himself into the piss bucket, he proudly proclaimed "It's good to be the king!"

CHAPTER 29

Have a nice day

It was May, and Washington DC was at its most beautiful. Everywhere you looked there were flowering trees, beautifully manicured gardens carpeted with tulips and daffodils and all the other cheerful, brightly colored spring flowers. The wooded areas were alive with the cacophony of the songs of birds declaring territorial rights and advertising for mates. For the past few weeks, there had been no big crises at Marbella and things had been going pretty smoothly.

Unfortunately, as the saying goes, all good things must come to an end. It was the day before Mr. & Mrs. Cooke's second wedding anniversary and, predictably, Mrs. Cooke had once again disappeared from Marbella. Her extended absences were becoming more frequent and this created a lot of tension in the house. Mr. Cooke understandably grew more and more irritable and downright explosive.

We were expecting Virginia's Governor Wilder for a meeting on the new stadium. Waiting for the governor, Mr. Cooke expectantly paced back and forth between the library and my office, restlessly shifting papers around and moving decorative things from one table top to another. He was in constant nervous motion which, in turn, was making me nervous. When he was in my office, he looked around in the closet but apparently couldn't find whatever it was he was looking for. Frustrated, he slammed the closet doors and growled "this is some place". Not wanting to call attention to myself, I kept quiet and tried to ignore him.

The houseman came into the library to deliver something and, for no apparent reason, Mr. Cooke called him a "stupid ass" over and over again. He even chewed out his general counsel who had arrived earlier to help him prepare for the important meeting.

Clearly, this was one of those days that required we all tiptoe around Cooke as carefully as possible, as if walking on the proverbial egg shells. All bets were off. It didn't matter if you were the houseman or executive assistant or the general counsel or even the Governor of Virginia. No one was safe today.

The governor finally arrived and, always the consummate politician, he made sure he cheerfully greeted every single one of us, house staff included, before he joined the meeting. I was relieved when the meeting finally began. I could then close my door and be sheltered in the limited safety of my office. I had had more than enough of Mr. Cooke for one day. I stayed at Marbella until the meeting ended, not long after my usual quitting time, and made a quick getaway.

CHAPTER 30

Fracas at the fortress

I opened the gate and entered the grounds of Marbella on the morning of Mr. & Mrs. Cooke's second wedding anniversary. No one was in sight except for the carpenter who had become a permanent fixture working on Marbella's never ending punch list. As soon as he laid eyes on me, he ran over and, barely able to contain his excitement, told me Mrs. Cooke had shot herself in the hand last night in Mr. Cooke's bathroom! Oh crap, I thought to myself, here we go again. What a freaking circus! What will it be next?

I took a moment to compose myself and, gathering as much courage as possible, I entered the house. I silently went through the now familiar routine of removing my shoes and putting on my slippers. I had decided that playing dumb would be the best approach. I entered the library on my way to my office and there was Mr. Cooke standing by his desk. I looked at him and, trying to sound as normal as possible, said "good morning Mr. Cooke". He returned the greeting and very calmly announced, all in one sentence, that he was going out, that Mrs. Cooke had shot herself in the hand and had broken a finger, and that she was in the hospital registered under the name of Jane Elliot. I acted shocked and told him how sorry I was to hear that and told him I hoped Mrs. Cooke was okay. He thanked me for my concern and left.

The local media were having a field day with this irresistible, juicy bit of news. It took precedence over all the real and much more important news. It was the only thing people wanted to talk about. All of us at Marbella knew the house would soon be inundated with reporters. We also knew it was just a matter of time before Mr. Cooke started calling every five minutes and would have all of us frantically jumping from one task to another. We all manned our battle stations and waited for the firestorm to begin.

It wasn't long before the house staff and I were caught in a barrage of Mr. Cooke's calls. He'd hang up and then call right back. His calls came in one after the other, as quickly as he could dial them. We felt like soldiers on the front line in an intense battle. First, he directed me to send the cook out to buy "six of the finest plums possible". Of course, it wasn't plum season, so there were no plums be found anywhere despite the cook's frantic one-and-a-half-hour search. And no one had the courage to tell Mr. Cooke he couldn't have his plums. About half an hour after the cook departed on his plum quest, Mr. Cooke told me he wanted the cook to make all kinds of special food for Mrs. Cooke RIGHT AWAY because she couldn't eat the hospital food, it was so awful. When I told him I'd have the cook get to work on the special food order as soon as he got back, he became furious because the cook wasn't back yet with the plums. (Hello! Mr. Cooke, I hate to tell you this but the cook can't be in two places at once! He's out looking for your PERFECT OUT OF SEASON plums!)

And then he turned his anger on me: it was suddenly my fault for not directing the cook to return IMMEDIATELY once he had found the plums . . . that the cook was out "galli-vanting" instead of coming straight back to Marbella. Who did he think the cook was, Butterfly McQueen in "*Gone With the Wind*", dilly dallying down the sidewalk and not knowin' nuthin' bout buyin' no plums? I couldn't believe he had made such an unfair assumption about a good, faithful employee who genuinely liked him (God only knew why) and worked his ass off for him. I recalled how, just a short while ago, Mr. Cooke had told me about how he was always amazed at people who "jump to conclusions so much that they get hernias". Who was jumping to conclusions now?

Things went from bad to worse. It was impossible to describe how I felt sitting there, completely helpless, at my desk, with Mr. Cooke spewing his endless anger and frustration at me, his easiest and most convenient target. He literally called me every two minutes and demanded everything AT ONCE, knowing I couldn't possibly deliver because the person he wanted was still out looking for plums. And he still insisted it was all my fault.

The only thing I could do was laugh at the absurdity of it all. Mr. Cooke got people so jumpy and riled up that even the simplest of operations would become totally comedic and outrageously silly. Charlie Chaplin would have been impressed. What should have been a simple task for any normal person, like going to the dentist for example, became a logistical nightmare of huge proportions whenever it involved Mrs. Cooke. The simple appointment would blow up into a major project of the most intense nature, often requiring three or four people scrambling about to make sure everything happened the way it should, while the totally disinterested Mrs. Cooke would just sit there and do nothing and wait for someone to ship her off in the limo. I often thought that must be what it was like for the secret service to get the President somewhere.

Later that afternoon, after all the special food had been frantically prepared and delivered to the hospital, Mr. Cooke called me and asked "you gave Kent Farms the number to reach me, right?" Oh God. That was a loaded question and it caught me completely off guard. I had a millisecond to think it through before I answered him. It was a trap that would give him another opportunity to give me hell. All the usual alarms went off in my head and I knew that no matter what my answer was it would be dead wrong. Mr. Cooke had never told me to call Kent Farms and, by now, I had learned the hard way that he was very sensitive about any of the staff communicating with each other about him and Mrs. Cooke (much of the time this forced us to try to do our jobs with our hands tied behind our backs). Also, the secretaries at Kent Farms told me Mr. Cooke had been in touch with them earlier that day.

So, after I worked through all of this in my head at lightning speed, I told him “no sir”. Wrong answer! I had fallen into the trap and had to endure another endless, merciless reprimand. Caught by the grey area again! Damned if you do and damned if you don’t! It had been such a long day and I was fried, I just couldn’t take anymore. Mr. Cooke had behaved horribly. He had lashed out at everyone. He had been absolutely at his worst, even more so than after the Super Bowl. He had even called the cook a “stupid black bastard” after everything he had done for Mr. Cooke that day.

Towards the end of the day Mr. Cooke called me from his car on his way home from the hospital and kept me on the phone the entire time while he mostly talked to himself and worked through his thoughts. He started in on me again and, pushed to my limits, I said “I guess I’m just not the secretary you thought I was Mr. Cooke”. I thought what the heck, I’m done anyway, so I continued and tried to justify something I had done earlier. He interrupted me, yelling “SHUT UP”. He then started talking about doing things in a certain way, that if he had done things my way he’d have “ended up being a stupid stenographer”. Oh, I thought to myself, you’re not getting away with that one, Mr. Cooke. My gloves are coming off, you bastard. I asked him “Is that what you think I am, Mr. Cooke, a stupid stenographer?” After a two second pause (during which I wondered if he was thinking to himself “uh oh, I might have gone a little too far this time”) he thoughtfully said “noooo” and then wormed his way out of it. He then said to me “you are afraid of hurting people’s feelings, aren’t you?” and I said “yes sir”. He replied, in a more determined voice, “I don’t give a damn, I want to progress!”

Once Mr. Cooke returned to Marbella, I was able to leave. After I closed the door behind me I wanted to run as fast as I could and get the hell out of there. I made it to my car and quickly jumped in, so thankful to be in MY space and, for the first time all day, not have to answer to anyone.

My reflections on the day? There are people in this world who never get into any sort of trouble. And there are people in this world who are accidents looking for places to happen. Mr. & Mrs. Cooke were those kind of people. I never knew what to expect any more when I came to work. Anything was possible. It was like looking in on young children, discovering what sort of trouble they had made for themselves after being left alone all night.

More and more with each new day, my anxiety would build as I made the now dreaded drive to Marbella. Once I parked my car and left behind the safety and security of my personal world and walked through the gate into Marbella, I felt as though I was entering the gates of hell. The only thing missing was Cerberus.

Mr. Cooke had brought Mrs. Cooke home from the hospital this morning and I was very relieved to find him in a much kinder frame of mind. It was as though he had got all of his nastiness out of himself yesterday. He was a much happier man with Mrs. Cooke back home and in his bed. Of course, he had the servants jumping all over the place to make sure she had every possible comfort and then some.

The drama of the gun mishap continued and followed Mrs. Cooke from the hospital to Marbella. By mid-day, the reporters started showing up at the gate, effectively imprisoning all of us at Marbella. Normally, I would take a break and go to my car and just relax for ten minutes or so and listen to the birds and get some fresh air. That was now impossible.

Early in the afternoon, detectives came to Marbella to begin their investigation and get Mrs. Cooke's statement. With great pomp and circumstance, this all took place in the Cookes' bedroom where Mrs. Cooke, regally propped up in the bed, surrounded by pillows and Chanel in her lap, held court. Present were Mr. Cooke, his attorney and three detectives. I was called in to type Mrs. Cooke's statement on a little table and typewriter which had been set up at the foot of the bed. It was a production worthy of Cecil B DeMille.

My work day over, I left Marbella and made my way through the throng of reporters to my car, ignoring their questions. They reminded me of blood hungry Alaskan mosquitoes, worked up into a feeding frenzy, looking for fresh insight into the sensational story. I wanted to tell them all to go find something more important and newsworthy to report on.

CHAPTER 31

Please please please introduce me!

The next day, things seemed to have quieted down at Marbella, if that was possible. I was greeted by a TV film crew on my way into Marbella who asked me if I was a visitor or if I worked there. I ignored them as politely as I could while I opened the gate and entered Marbella.

After I got settled in at my desk, Mr. Cooke told me he was accompanying Mrs. Cooke to the hospital for her first physical therapy session on her finger. I had to laugh to myself that he felt she needed him to go with her. It was a finger for chrissake! Even more ridiculous was that she came home with a pretty pink splint and all kinds of fancy bandages all the way to her elbow. I thought of the thousands of little girls who would be jealous of such a bandage for their little booboos! But, more importantly, Mr. Cooke was in good spirits and that's all I cared about.

At Mr. Cooke's request, Coach Gibbs came to Marbella that afternoon. I was really excited at the chance to finally meet the revered Redskins head coach. I knew he had arrived and he was in the library with Mr. Cooke but I couldn't see him because my door was closed. I finally had my big chance when Mr. Cooke buzzed me and asked me to bring in some papers. I couldn't wait to go in and see Coach Gibbs in person! I gathered the requested papers and opened the door and there was Coach Gibbs sitting opposite Mr. Cooke at that big sea of a desk. I carefully set the papers down on the desk by Mr. Cooke. I hesitated ever so briefly, foolishly thinking that at any moment Mr. Cooke might extend me the courtesy of introducing me to the famous coach. I was completely ignored. Disappointed and humiliated, I returned to my office and closed the door.

Even on the rare occasions that my co-workers from Kent Farms came to Marbella, introductions were never made, so I never was able to match a face with a voice. Further, we were never allowed to call each other by our first names. Instead, we were required to call each other "Mrs., Miss or Mr. X". And, when we had to call each other it was a big no-no to begin the call with the usual and customary "hello, how are you?". If we did so we were subject to severe reprimand by Mr. Cooke because, in his words, it was a waste of time and nobody really cares how someone is when they ask. Instead, we were expected to dial the number and when the phone was answered we were to get right to the reason for the call – NO social chitchat! This was so foreign to me. I never got comfortable doing that. I thought we must be the only people on the planet who were required to do this. And I didn't think anyone would believe me if I told them.

Later in the day, after Coach Gibbs left, Mr. Cooke dictated a thank you message, to be sent out over Mrs. Cooke's signature, to everyone who had sent her flowers while she was in the hospital (for one day!). Heaven forbid she should write anything by herself. I soon learned that Mr. Cooke composed all of Mrs. Cooke's letters and returned her phone calls. I could only think he did that because she wasn't the most intelligent or eloquent person and he didn't want anyone to know that. They were such an odd couple. Aside from the obvious (her job was to get all dolled up and be his arm candy in public and his job was to be the ATM), I couldn't figure out how in the world they could possibly be happy together. They had nothing in common. Intelligence and proper use of the English language were of paramount importance to Mr. Cooke, to the point he wouldn't hesitate to correct anyone, no matter who or how important they were, on their use of the English language. Mrs. Cooke was totally lacking in those areas. I had never heard her say anything that impressed me, nor did I ever even see her with a book. The closest I ever saw her get to reading was to look through fashion magazines. Shopping and nightclubbing appeared to be her favorite activities. Armed with Mr. Cooke's credit card, she was a force to be reckoned with. She was also 40 years younger than Mr. Cooke. Normally, I wouldn't have cared about such a thing. But in this case I did care a great deal because Mr. Cooke's happiness and state of mind, which seemed to always be hanging precariously in the balance, affected me directly.

CHAPTER 32

Reporters, police, Redskins & ex-wives, and a good day to keep in my back pocket

By the third day after the shot heard round the world, only one or two film crews continued their stakeout at Marbella, still hoping to garner an undisclosed morsel about Mrs. Cooke's mishap with the gun. Rain showers soon discouraged them and they finally disappeared.

The police returned to Marbella to continue their investigation of the shooting and also take photos of Mr. Cooke's bathroom and dressing room where it had all happened. Mr. Cooke quickly handed them off to me and I escorted them to his bathroom and stayed there while they conducted their investigation: photos of the room, photos of the bloodstains on the carpeting and blood samples from the carpet. You would have thought someone had been murdered. I was relieved when they finally left and I could get back to my normal routine.

The Redskins were back in town, each player's well earned vacation time now just a pleasant memory. Mini-camp was set for next weekend at Redskin Park. I was very surprised to receive a handwritten invitation from Mr. Cooke, inviting me to attend the informal practice and barbecue that would follow. This was the first time he ever did anything nice or thoughtful for me and I was excited! I would finally get to meet the coaches and players! I thanked Mr. Cooke and accepted his invitation.

Today, Mr. Cooke was harassed by his ex-wife, Suzanne, whom I was required by Mr. Cooke to refer to as "The Bitch" (none of the staff were allowed to refer to her by her name). Just recently, she had begun calling repeatedly and sending letters to Mr. Cooke and making accusations about inappropriate behavior by Mrs. Cooke. Understandably, this made Mr. Cooke crazy. Ugh! There was no relief! It went from one problem to another! Earlier this week it was Mrs. Cooke getting shot in the finger. Now it was "The Bitch's" constant harassment. What would it be next week? And, for the record, having to refer to my boss's ex-wife as "The Bitch", while I was speaking to him, was right off the planet Mars for me. Why not just label them "Mrs. Cooke I", "Mrs. Cooke II", "Mrs. Cooke III" and "Mrs. Cooke IV & V"???

God only knew how badly I needed the coming weekend. The only thing I wanted to do was go to bed and pull the covers over my head. I needed to escape!

On Sunday afternoon, I drove to Redskin Park. From the parking lot I could see that tents and chairs and tables had been set up alongside of the practice fields. Several guests had already arrived. I introduced myself to the front office staff who were manning the entrance and they were happy to meet me. It was so nice to be around "normal" people for a change. The head PR guy escorted me down to the fields and introduced me to a few people so I would feel more comfortable. Most of the guests were Mr. Cooke's friends so I kept a pretty low profile for fear of saying something wrong and having it come back and bite me. A "practice", mostly just for show, was already under way.

At first I had been afraid Mr. Cooke might treat me the same way he did at Marbella and embarrass me, but my fear was completely unfounded. I was treated with the same respect as all of the other guests. Curiously, at a Redskins function, there were no rankings or privilege among guests. We were all fans, our common denominator the Redskins. I was seated along the sideline where I watched the practice. It was an incredible experience to be that close and watch and hear the players be themselves. I felt really special and realized how privileged I was to be included in this special day with the reigning Super Bowl champion Washington Redskins.

Much like any simple dress rehearsal, everyone was relaxed and light-hearted. The players ran several drills among the offense, defense and special teams and then scrimmaged a little bit. After the practice, we all moved into the tents for the barbecue. I couldn't believe it as I sat there amongst all of the great Redskins players: Jeff Bostic, Ricky Ervins, Darrell Green, Art Monk, Joe Jacoby, Charles Mann. . . wow! I couldn't recall ever being exposed to so much testosterone at one time! I had gone from famine to feast! Sensory overload! All the players were very nice to me, especially after I told them I was Mr. Cooke's assistant. Ha! They all probably felt sorry for me and already had a pool going for how long I'd last.

Alongside of the barbecue tent, there was a table set up on which the Redskins' three huge, sterling silver Super Bowl trophies, each one polished to perfection, were displayed. Mr. Cooke proudly stood behind the trophies and posed with his guests as the team photographer snapped away with his camera. I stood off to the side and watched but didn't dare ask for a picture. Then Mr. Cooke saw me and I couldn't believe it when he waived at me to come join him for a commemorative photo.

This had been one of those very rare days that were so special and good that they really helped me get through all the bad ones. I would keep the memory of this day in my back pocket and pull it out whenever I began to be overwhelmed by the temptation to quit my job.

CHAPTER 33

I picked it out just for you

One day, Mr. Cooke and I were working together in the library when he suddenly remembered it was a friend‘s birthday. Without giving it any further thought, he got up from his desk and disappeared into his bedroom suite. A minute or two later he reappeared, carrying one of his Hermes ties — complete with stain. He set it down on his desk and told me to go into the closet in my office and take out one of the trademark rust colored Hermes gift boxes. I retrieved the box and set it onto his desk next to the soiled tie. Mr. Cooke then placed the tie in the box and wrote a note on one of his luxuriously thick, engraved cards, the trademark calling card of the privileged. He had me wrap the gift and then instructed me to have it and the card delivered to his friend that afternoon.

Now I knew what all those empty Hermes and Tiffany's boxes in my supply closet were for! I couldn't get over what I had just witnessed. I didn't think I, and many others for that matter, would ever come close to understanding the enigma that Mr. Cooke truly was. And what would his friend think when he took the tie out of the box and saw the stain! I couldn't wait to see what Mr. Cooke would put in the light blue Tiffany's boxes.

CHAPTER 34

Can you hear me now?

Mr. Cooke was very tired and edgy this morning. The houseman, the cook and I all needed to stay on our toes and be very careful not to do anything that would set him off. It was one of those "egg shell" days. Even though it was 80 degrees and sunny outside, Mr. Cooke was in bed with his newspapers and a roaring fire in the fireplace. He was out late the night before, to a big dinner at the Canadian Embassy which had also been attended by President & Mrs. Bush. He told me he had had a "marvelous" time. Unfortunately, for the first time since her shooting accident, and after all the special care and attention Mr. Cooke had showered upon her, Mrs. Cooke was again absent from Marbella.

I was in the kitchen when Mr. Cooke buzzed for one of the servants. The cook was out grocery shopping and the houseman was buffing the marble floor, so I answered the phone and said "kitchen, Miss Crozier speaking". He obviously couldn't hear me very well because he thought I was the houseman. I said "no sir, this is Miss Crozier. The cook is out grocery shopping and the houseman is buffing the floor. Would you like me to get the houseman for you?" After one or two seconds, Mr. Cooke said "This is who? I dialed the kitchen". I explained once more what I was doing in the kitchen and why I answered the kitchen phone and he snapped "Well why didn't you say so in the first place!". Okaaaay. I hung up the phone, silently laughing to myself, and asked the houseman to go to Mr. Cooke.

Mr. Cooke's mood seemed to improve as the day wore on. After staying in bed until about 1:00 o'clock, he put on a short-sleeved cotton shirt and white shorts and, wearing his trademark wrap-around, oversized black sunglasses, he parked himself alongside the pool for some sun. From the fire place to the pool!

Before he got dressed and went outside, I made several trips to his bedside with messages and things he had requested. He was quiet and contemplative and just wanted to talk. He asked me what I thought about Mrs. Cooke's older son and his laziness (he had no job, no hobbies to speak of and would sleep away the entire day if he could get away with it.) All the familiar alarms went off in my head and I knew I had to carefully think through my response before I made it. Speaking in an obtuse manner was a challenge for me. All my life, I had never been able to ignore the elephant in the room; if there was one there I was gonna talk about it. I only knew how to say it like it was. On the other hand, my instincts told me it wasn't a good idea to express opinions about any aspects of Mr. Cooke's personal life, especially to the man himself, because I knew it could only lead to trouble. So, after pondering my answer and thinking "oh man, here goes nothing", I told him I would be very frank and candid. I carefully cast my response out there like a line on a fly rod. I said the boy didn't know the meaning of responsibility or the value of a dollar; that he was exposed to great wealth and privileges and felt a sense of entitlement to all of the things his mother and Mr. Cooke enjoyed.

My answer complete and hanging there in the atmosphere of Mr. Cooke's bedroom, I remained silent and waited for Mr. Cooke's reaction. He stared straight ahead at the fire for a couple of minutes, then looked at me and said he agreed with me. I was just starting to feel smug and confident but then it all backfired when he asked me to "stay on top of things and make sure the boy did his assigned chores each day". Oh crap! This was a new trap I had unwittingly fallen into, because I knew *nobody* – not even Mr. Cooke or Mrs. Cooke could control the two unmanageable boys. And if they couldn't control them, how was I supposed to? I wondered where this new responsibility was listed on my job description.

After 2 ½ hours, Mr. Cooke was still out by the pool in the hot sun. The temperature had risen into the high 80s and the humidity was building. Like the devil himself, the hotter it got the more he loved it.

Mr. Cooke had summoned Charley Casserly, the Redskins General Manager, to come to Marbella to meet with him. When Charley arrived, he was shown to the oven-like patio. The poor guy was wearing dark slacks, a tie and a jacket and I just knew he was miserable out there. There was no umbrella to shield him from the sun and, in true form, Mr. Cooke was completely oblivious to Casserly's discomfort, even though rivers of sweat were pouring down his face. They were soon joined by Mr. John and Mr. Cooke asked me to find the houseman to serve them wine. The houseman was out picking up Mrs. Cooke's younger son from school, so I retrieved the requested bottle, opened it and served the wine, complete with the little silver tray. A new skill for my resume!

CHAPTER 35

Never assume it will be an easy day

Shortly after I arrived at Marbella, Mr. Cooke informed me he was going to spend the day in Middleburg. I was thrilled at hearing this. Hooray! He hadn't been to the farm for two months and I would be very happy to see the chaos move from Marbella to Kent Farms for the day. I could picture the staff at Kent Farms rushing around like idiots to make sure everything was ready for his royal highness. Unfortunately, he took his time and it seemed like forever before he finally got into his BMW and left.

From out of nowhere, before he left, Mr. Cooke angrily confronted me, demanding to know why I didn't tell him Mrs. Cooke's new phone directory for her Jaguar had been delivered from Kent Farms. I was surprised by this because he had never cared or shown any interest in the updating process of all the car phone directories which was carried out by the Kent Farms staff. On and on he went about how I should have told him the directory was back in her car. Ayayayayay! The rules must have changed again!

I hadn't yet recovered from the directory debacle when Mr. Cooke asked me if I had his ruler. I said "no sir" and offered him my ruler and inquired (just for the sake of making conversation — never a smart thing to do with Mr. Cooke) if his ruler was missing, to which he replied "noooo, I just thought I would ask where my ruler was".

Mr. Cooke finally left for Kent Farms and did not return to Marbella until 5 pm. I was working in my office, enjoying the peace and quiet, when he walked into the library, accompanied by Mr. John. He was completely out of sorts. NOTHING was done right! Door closers that he had ordered to be mounted on the door between the library and my office had been installed during the day but according to Mr. Cooke they weren't on right. Then he asked me why I let the carpenter put them on that way. I thought "what the hell do I know about door closers and construction?!". I told him I didn't know anything about construction and he proclaimed "you're learning now, aren't you?!" He then proceeded to yell out, every time someone opened his door "WATCH OUT, THAT DOOR WILL KILL YOU". He then called and ordered the carpenter to return to Marbella "AT ONCE" and "FIX THE GODDAMN FUCKING DOOR STOPPERS!!!".

Oh my god! I was dying, this was beyond funny. I guess I was finally getting used to his tantrums and seeing the sick, humorous side of it all. I was learning how to survive in the kingdom of Cooke.

To make the day complete, a new washing machine was to have been delivered and installed that afternoon while Mr. Cooke was in Middleburg. His architect — now the unfortunate, appointed-on-the-spot "handyman", thought he would have a repair person check out the current washer to confirm a new washer was really needed and, sure enough, the repair man determined that a simple repair was all that was needed.

I, the unfortunate messenger of the unwanted news, called Mr. Cooke in his car to tell him that instead of a new washer being delivered, a repair person was working on the old washer. This was not what he wanted to hear! He called the architect and ordered him to have the <u>new</u> washer delivered "IMMEDIATELY, TODAY, AND IT IS TO BE HOOKED UP TODAY AS WELL, REGARDLESS OF THE LATE HOUR". Now, because the unfortunate architect had told Mr. Cooke the day before that the new washer would be installed "tomorrow" (which was now today), Mr. Cooke was holding him to his word, saying "'tomorrow' starts at 12:01 am and goes until 11:59 pm 'tomorrow' night and if you said it was ok for the washer to be hooked up 'tomorrow', then it could still be hooked up at 11:59 'tomorrow' night!" As usual, Mr. Cooke got his way and a special delivery and special installation of the new washer was completed just before midnight.

Also after Mr. Cooke returned from Middleburg, he went off at me for calling the architect by his first name (as I had been doing for the past six months, but just not in front of Mr. Cooke). He asked me if he had heard correctly that I had done so. I said "yes sir". He said "well, you should not". Then he turned to his son and threw his hands up in the air and said "this first name stuff is getting out of hand!" Yeah, well, this "first name stuff" was so weird to me I didn't even know how to react to it. I just ignored Mr. Cooke's lecture and returned to work.

What a day! And it was supposed to be an easy day with the boss in Middleburg! For the zillionth time, I began wondering why I was still there and putting up with all this crazy nonsense and thought about how nice it would be to work in a normal place where people were kind and there was none of this ridiculous bullshit. It was such an easy place to go when the pressure became too much. Whenever Mr. Cooke made up his mind that nothing was going to be right, that's exactly what happened. He made his own rules and they were subject to change from day to day. He made it no secret that he marched to his own drum. When he laughed, you laughed. When he was pissed off, you ducked and covered. He loved to make people jump, run and sweat, all at his whim.

CHAPTER 36

Take a message

Today, Mr. Cooke was in an "ok" mood which was certainly an improvement over his behavior of the day before. However, he was still sarcastic to the point of making me crazy. At about 10:30 am, Mrs. Cooke's mother called. I didn't know if Mrs. Cooke was up yet, so I asked Mr. Cooke if it was ok to put the call through. He said no, that the rule of thumb was to tell all callers for Mrs. Cooke (apparently including her own mother) that she was not at home and to take a message. I wondered what the big mystery was and why she couldn't take calls like everyone else. But things weren't normal there, so I did what I was told and didn't think anymore about it.

The highlight of the day for me was when Coach Gibbs returned to Marbella for another meeting with Mr. Cooke. Before he arrived I asked Mr. Cooke if he would introduce me to Gibbs as I hadn't met him yet. To my surprise, Mr. Cooke agreed to do so! As Coach Gibbs entered Marbella, Mr. Cooke had me come into the library and wait with him for the famous coach come into his office, at which time the much anticipated introduction was made. It was a thrill to finally meet the coach. That one small favor from Mr. Cooke gave a tremendous boost to my spirits and I floated through the rest of the day.

CHAPTER 37

Another eggshell day

Today at Marbella, things got off to a scary start. When I arrived, I found the staff very anxious and nervous, doing the by now familiar eggshell shuffle. I learned that, outside of sneaking in quietly to take her younger son with her, Mrs. Cooke had not returned to Marbella since yesterday morning. And, to make matters even more tense, anonymous phone calls were coming in about Mrs. Cooke and inappropriate behavior.

Mr. Cooke was as mad as a bear woken up in the middle of winter. He wanted to fight with everybody about everything. First, he told the cook to look for another job because he didn't like his work habits. This made no sense to me because he had told me over and over again that the cook was worth his weight in gold and that he would trust his life with him. I couldn't believe that Mr. Cooke would make such a big mistake. I knew the cook really cared about him and that he was extremely dependable and an excellent employee; he always put in 110% and then some. Plus he was good at keeping the houseman in line which was a huge bonus for me.

Wow, if he was treating the cook like this, I wondered what was in store for me. I certainly didn't want to give him any reason to be upset with me. I could be the most careful person in the world and do nothing wrong but he would still find or make up something so he could come after me. It was a very scary feeling, working in his house, knowing he was watching every move I made.

I was starting to wonder what sort of effect all of the stress was having on my body. I knew it wasn't good for me. Quitting time, 6:30 pm, finally rolled around without incident. Time to go! What a relief to get in my car and make my escape. Whew! I had survived another day!

CHAPTER 38

I know something you don't know . . .

The Governor of Virginia was at Marbella again yesterday for another meeting with Mr. Cooke about the new stadium. The governor never failed to find me, shake my hand and say hello. He must have instinctually known I was a Virginia voter. After months of meetings and discussions with various politicians and local officials, Mr. Cooke was moving closer and closer to finally making a deal for the future home of the Washington Redskins' new stadium. He was very anxious to tie up all the loose ends and plan a press conference on the stadium site to formally announce the location. The local media had been full of speculation on the stadium's location. Would it be in Virginia, Maryland or DC? If they only knew what I knew!

CHAPTER 39

Just another day at the office

Things were crazy this morning. Mrs. Cooke, who had eventually returned to Marbella after another one of her countless absences, had an appointment this morning with her hand surgeon. Trying to get her to any appointment on time was like trying to herd cats. She was completely oblivious to time and place, nor was she interested. As a result, staff suffered whenever she had to be somewhere at a certain time.

After they finally left, Mr. Cooke called me from the limo and told me to call the doctor's office to let them know they were running late and that I was to give them all of Mrs. Cooke's information over the phone so at least the paperwork would be done by the time they arrived. Yikes! I had only seen bits and pieces of Mrs. Cooke's personal information scattered about in different files, among which I had noticed at least three different birth dates – on official records! Mr. Cooke asked me if I had all the info and, not really wanting to commit, I said I "thought" I did because one thing I'd learned with him was that you never said yes without being 150% sure. But this didn't work either. He snapped at me in his nasty voice "WELL DO YOU OR DON'T YOU HAVE THE INFORMATION BECAUSE IF YOU DON'T I'LL CALL MY SECRETARY AT KENT FARMS AND HAVE HER TAKE CARE OF IT". I responded "I believe I have the information sir" and he said "that's better Miss Crozier".

What I really wanted to say to him was "If you could get that irresponsible, apathetic, lazy wife of yours to get herself to the doctor's office on time, she would be able to fill out her own freaking paperwork like everyone else does!" I had no respect for Mrs. Cooke. She was a troublemaker and caused everyone a lot of pain. She was cold and disconnected and those hard, black eyes of hers gave me the heebie jeebies.

Frantically, I searched through the files and grabbed all the information I could find. Then I called the doctor's office and told them, as Mr. Cooke had directed, that I was Mrs. Cooke's "private secretary" and gave them her information. When they asked for her birth date, I put the three different "official" dates in front of me and did the old "eenie meenie miney mo" and gave them the "mo" date. I was very humiliated at having to introduce myself as that woman's private secretary. Things had sunk to a new level.

Later that day, in the afternoon, the gruesome twosome returned and entered the house, verbally sparring with each other, and ended up in the library. Before I knew it, an all out, no holds barred fight had erupted between them and, not for the first time, I found myself an unwilling listener, captive in my office. I had never heard people fight like that before! I wanted to run out of the house and get away as fast as I could.

The quarrel continued. At one point, Mr. Cooke pulled his older stepson into the middle of the argument, ordering him to come to his side, and then he yelled to Mrs. Cooke that her son was on his side and wanted to stay with him. There was a lot of chaos and yelling; I heard Mr. Cooke yell "you're not going to punch me in the nose" and then he shouted over and over "get out", "get out" . . . and Mrs. Cooke shouted "no", "no", "no". I was horrified and sat there frozen at my desk. I even covered up my ears and willed them not to hear anymore of the horrible fight. Never in my life had I seen or heard such an explosive and hateful argument between a husband and a wife.

Right in the middle of it all, Mr. Cooke told me to place a call to his second wife, with whom he was still on good terms. I had to leave a message for her and I quickly told him that. He said "fine". About 15 minutes later, as the argument continued, Mrs. Cooke No. 2 returned the call and I put it through. Mr. Cooke took the call but spoke only for a moment. Then he stormed into my office and looked at me as if I were crazy and bellowed at me "YOU HAD TO BE OUT OF YOUR MIND TO PUT A CALL LIKE THAT THROUGH AT A TIME LIKE THAT".

Huh??? What??? This was so ridiculous that now I started to wonder if they were playing some sort of sick joke on me or something. What sort of shenanigans was he up to now? After a minute or two, I realized he may have done that just so he could figure out a way to blame the whole argument on me.

Did Mr. Cooke really think I enjoyed having to sit in my office and listen while he and Mrs. Cooke had such fierce arguments? To listen to them scream at each other? At least they could have moved from the library into the privacy of their bedroom so no one would have to hear them. I longed to work in a place where things were normal, where I wouldn't have to witness vicious arguments and where I could actually call people by their first names!

CHAPTER 40

It's just a Monopoly game

The day after the terrible fight between Mr. & Mrs. Cooke, returning to work was like an out of body experience for me. My body was following the familiar routine, but I really didn't want to go there. It was the last place in the world I wanted to be. I was relieved to find that things seemed to be ok between them. Mr. Cooke had even rearranged his office and made some changes in the furniture. Then he had all the wood simonized and he personally supervised, while the houseman and his older stepson applied the elbow grease. The day passed quietly, for which I was ever so grateful.

That evening, Mr. Cooke called me at home just to tell me that he had planned another meeting with Virginia's Governor for Monday regarding the new stadium. He told me "we're gonna get something done this time". I agreed with him that it sure would be nice to get the stadium agreement finalized. He said "good bye" and hung up.

Also that evening I read an article in the newspaper about charges being dropped against Mr. Cooke for being in possession of a gun in the District of Columbia, his main defense being that he didn't know he had it in the house. Shaking my head in disgust, I wondered at how easy it was for the wealthy and privileged to just flash their "get out of jail free" card and walk away from their messes.

CHAPTER 41

Chaos as usual

The next several days were uneventful, except for frequent visits by the governor as things progressed steadily toward acquisition of the Virginia site for the new stadium.

At about 4 pm, Mr. Cooke got a phone call and, as soon as he hung up, he looked at me and said "it's out", meaning that the Potomac Yard stadium site had finally been leaked. He didn't seem upset at this; rather, he seemed kind of excited. I started to think the "leak" had been intentional. At that point things started hopping and he was thrilled to be back on top again. He called everyone, including the governor who was in Africa, to make sure they knew just what to say when asked about the site, that Potomac Yard was one of six northern Virginia sites being considered by Mr. Cooke.

The excitement continued to build into the next day and once again, to his complete and utter delight, Mr. Cooke was the talk of the town. There were front page articles in all the local newspapers about the Potomac Yard site. It was decided the formal announcement would be made at a lavish press conference at Potomac Yard on July 7.

A couple of days later, I arrived at Marbella to find Mr. Cooke extremely irritable. He got angry when I gave him a message that the houseman, who was on an errand, had called for him. I had tried to tell him earlier, but he said he didn't want any messages, so I held onto it for just another 5 minutes before I tried again. When the houseman originally called, Mr. Cooke was on the phone and normal procedure was to take a message. But now, all I heard was "OH MISS CROZIER, WHAT HAVE YOU DONE?" "YOU SHOULD HAVE INTERRUPTED MY CALL!" What a way to start the day.

The chaos continued, with the smallest of tasks becoming major productions. Mrs. Cooke had an 11:00 am dentist appointment and we all knew what that meant. OF COURSE she was late. OF COURSE Mr. Cooke got involved. And then her mother got involved. First, Mr. Cooke had me call the dentist to say Mrs. Cooke was going to be late — but that she was on her way (bullshit!). At 11 o'clock she was still sitting there in the library mindlessly babbling on about nothing and sipping her coffee (the dentist's office was 30 minutes away). Then Mr. Cooke had me call the dentist so he could talk to him.

Now, while all of this was going on, Mrs. Cooke's car was going into the shop for several days. Another car was being brought over from Kent Farms for her to use, but the phone in it didn't work. So, there were several calls going back and forth, with the phone technician promising Mr. Cooke that he'd drive to where Mrs. Cooke had her dentist appointment so he could fix the phone. And, if that wasn't enough, there were workmen at Marbella for ongoing construction projects, along with the crew of landscapers who had come to do their weekly work. So, there was General Cooke surrounded by his soldiers and playing the role to the max.

We didn't get far into the day when the vacuum cleaners (both of them!) decided to die. I took one cleaner outside and wasn't surprised to find that it was completely clogged with dog hair. After I got rid of the offending wads of hair and put the cleaner back together, it worked fine. The other vacuum cleaner needed its handle replaced. This was taken care of when Mr. Cooke, who was a master at wielding his name and power (after all, who in DC wouldn't bend over backwards for the owner of their beloved Redskins?), personally called the local Hoover rep who dropped everything and came running straight to Marbella and replaced the handle at no charge. I had to laugh at the irony of this and wondered if I would have gotten the same treatment had it been my vacuum cleaner.

So on and on went the Cooke merry-go-round that day. A real three ring circus.

CHAPTER 42

A long day with Mr. Cooke

The big press conference was only a couple of weeks away and the plans and meetings grew more intense. Today there was a big meeting with the bankers. They were very close to closing the deal with Mr. Cooke for the financing of the new stadium. I watched him as he prepared for the important meeting, joking one minute and snapping the next. The bankers arrived and, after a brief meeting in the library, off they went in Mr. Cooke's limo to see the new Redskin Park in Ashburn, VA, which was nearing completion, and then to the Potomac Yard stadium site.

Shortly after they left, the cook went to do the grocery shopping, as he did every Tuesday. Of course, 15 minutes after the cook left, Mr. Cooke called for him. I told him where the cook had gone and he almost lost it (he probably would have if he didn't have a car full of bankers he was trying to impress). Obviously struggling to keep his temper in check, he quietly growled into the phone "HOW COULD YOU DO THAT TO ME, WOMAN?". He said he wanted the cook to prepare a luncheon for his and the bankers' return to Marbella at 2:00 o'clock. I told Mr. Cooke I'd track the cook down and have him return to the house at once to prepare the lunch. I thought "gee Mr. Cooke, forgive your cook and me for not getting our crystal balls out and reading your mind that you wanted a special lunch prepared for everyone!". So now I had to round up the cook and tell him to get his butt back to Marbella on the double! I called the market and the manager found the cook and gave him my message. Ugh!

The cook returned to Marbella and he threw together a very nice lunch and had it all ready for Mr. Cooke and the bankers when they returned at 2:00 o'clock. As soon as Mr. Cooke came into the library, still not satisfied, he pointed his finger at me (!) and accused me of not having enough coffee prepared (hmm, when did I become the cook?) and also for not having a certain table in the library all cleared off for them to have their lunch on. Now how was I supposed to know that? I wondered what he would blame me for next, the weather? If only I were as powerful as Cooke seemed to think I was!

I often wondered if anyone ever noticed that I never took lunch hours. I was never thanked for going the extra mile and I wondered why I bothered. It was not my habit to take a lunch hour and also my nature to always do the best I could, no matter how menial the task. I thought I should probably make an effort to become more of a hard ass and take my lunch breaks no matter what.

Ah, there was nothing like spending a nice long day with Mr. Cooke. At around 5:15 pm, he asked me for the handwritten yellow legal sheet from which he had dictated the first draft of his stadium site announcement that morning. He knew I didn't have it because normal procedure — per his direction — was to shred ALL yellow sheets of handwritten notes once the draft had been typed. To cover his own ass, he was now saying he told me this morning that it was important and that I should have kept it. Ayayay!!! He never said any such thing to me! I was getting that horrible, insides turning to ice feeling again. I knew things were about to get ugly. I told him I was pretty sure I had shredded it to which he responded, or actually growled, "IF YOU DID I WILL KILL YOU WITH MY BARE HANDS", to which I replied "well Mr. Cooke I'm sure I did shred it", to which he then growled "THEN I'LL KILL YOU WITH MY BARE HANDS, CHEERFULLY".

I was ready to tell him "then have at it because I only followed your rules" when a miracle happened! He was called to the phone which gave me a moment to cool down and try to regain my composure. I sat there and waited for him to come storming back into my office with his hands on his hips and tower over me and look down at me and demand to know why in hell I shredded the bloody paper with the notes. The day had already grown too long and stressful and I was close to going over the edge.

By 6:10 he had not brought up the subject again. If he still wanted to kill me with his bare hands I decided I would tell him he needed another secretary. I knew he was itching for a fight but so was I. While I was waiting for him to kill me, he went and vented all his fury on the houseman whom I had heard he had decided to fire. The poor guy, I knew it would be a painful departure for him because Mr. Cooke would torture the hell out of him before he spat him out of Marbella.

I laid low until 6:30 and slipped out of Marbella, into the land of normal people.

CHAPTER 43

Weird stuff going on at your house? Just call FBI Guy

A lot of weird stuff was going on at Marbella. One of the boys' twin beds was full of shaving cream one night; Mrs. Cooke's Jaguar went missing between 3-6 am one night; there was missing liquor, etc. To get to the bottom of it all, Mr. Cooke decided to bring in an ex-FBI man to investigate. We were all questioned: executive assistant, house staff and the two boys. Personally, I was insulted that Mr. Cooke thought I had any role in any of the mischief. There was even some talk of each of us being asked to take lie detector tests. I made up my mind to draw the line then and there. If asked, I would refuse.

After FBI Guy finished questioning everyone and making observations and inspections, he uncovered the following: the houseman did the honors with the shaving cream in the bed in retaliation for the younger boy's covering his car with crushed oranges; the older had gone carousing in his mother's Jaguar; and the missing liquor was blamed on one of Mrs. Cooke's relatives who frequently visited at Marbella and apparently had a sense of entitlement to Mr. Cooke's well stocked liquor cabinet.

CHAPTER 44

Roast chicken and white mashed potatoes

Ever since FBI Guy made his findings, the last few days had been pretty quiet. Mr. Cooke was his usual cranky, demanding self. He seemed happiest when he was at his busiest and that was what he was at the moment. The big press conference and stadium announcement was now only seven days away. Yesterday he was really irritable until, after faxing countless drafts back and forth between Marbella and Redskin Park, he finally got the details for the press booklet just right. After he solved that problem, he was as happy and giddy as could be. You would have thought he was five years old and someone had given him the toy of his dreams. In this case it was a billionaire's toy: the new stadium for his Washington Redskins.

This morning, on my way to work, my car broke down and it had to be towed in for repairs. I called Mr. Cooke several times and kept him informed. I didn't arrive at Marbella until 12:15 but he was very understanding and when I apologized for any inconvenience I had caused him, he said right away that it wasn't my fault. Hmm, I thought, I finally wasn't being blamed for something.

Tasks today covered everything from preparing Mrs. Cooke's itinerary for her upcoming trip to Hawaii with her younger son, to working on Mr. Cooke's speech for the press conference. What really took the cake was Mr. Cooke asking <u>me</u> to make mashed potatoes for him before I left because it was the cook's day off and he told me the cook's mashed potatoes always came out grayish in color and he wanted <u>white</u> mashed potatoes! And oh, by the way, while you're at it, I'd like you to oversee the proper roasting of the chicken. OK, I had to laugh about this – what else could I do? I could appreciate being hungry for good mashed potatoes and roast chicken. Been there done that. Thank god I was a decent cook! What was next, laundry? I was soon on my way home, leaving behind a happy and contented Mr. Cooke with his white fluffy mashed potatoes and yummy roast chicken.

CHAPTER 45

"Have just a taste, dear, not a glass"

The press conference was just six days away and everyone was busy getting everything ready for the big day: Mr. Cooke's speech; invitation lists from the governor, the Potomac Yard owners and the Redskins; contents of press kits; et cetera. Lots of details! The fax machine was spitting out messages nonstop. Mr. Cooke was thriving on all the activity and loving every minute of it.

At the end of the day, Mr. Cooke uncorked what he called a $500 bottle of wine, a sumptuous Pauillac from a tiny little region in France. I couldn't believe it when he called me into the library and invited me to taste it. I walked over to the wet bar and selected a small glass and when I reached for the precious bottle, he cautioned me "just a taste though and not a glass". I very carefully poured myself a tiny bit of the precious wine. As Mr. Cooke watched me sip my little taste, I thought I had never tasted anything so smooth and warm and wonderful. It was like getting a hug from the inside out. Hmm, I thought, so this is what the rich folks drink!

CHAPTER 46

Instead of sending them to prison, they should make convicts work for Mr. Cooke

Today was a good day for Mr. Cooke. He was feeding off of all the activity and anticipation leading up to the press conference. It would be another big love fest with the media and Redskins fans, Jack Kent Cooke style.

Despite his good mood, he still found it necessary to give the servants a bad time. I thought the houseman was going to have a nervous breakdown. He looked like a scared dog that was afraid of being beaten, a steady stream of sweat pouring down his chubby black face as he did everything he could to stay out of the dangerous path of Mr. Cooke. The houseman had the unfortunate habit of doing things without first thinking them through and that drove Mr. Cooke bonkers.

Mr. Cooke got after the cook too. The cook had called in an order to the seafood shop for four red snapper filets for the Cookes' dinner that night and the houseman went to pick it up. The order got mixed up and they sent the houseman back with eight (not four) huge filets which ended up costing $62. Mr. Cooke was in the kitchen and opened the bag to inspect the fish. When he saw there were eight filets instead of four, he went crazy. He looked at the cook and said "well thanks a lot, I just gave you two Redskin shirts to give to your father and you turn around and do a thing like this. Now we'll have to freeze half of the fish and it won't be the same. It won't be fresh and the flavor won't be as good". And on and on he went about the fish.

Ignorant of the unfolding drama, I came into the kitchen to take care of something and right away Mr. Cooke drew me into the argument, looking for my support. I hated it when he did that because all it did was make everyone feel bad and it got me in trouble because I always told it like I saw it. So, when he asked for my opinion, I told him exactly what I thought (I still hadn't learned). I told him I thought that if the cook, not the houseman, had gone to pick up the fish he would have known right away that there was too much fish.

Uh oh. Big mistake. Mr. Cooke looked at me as though I was his worst enemy. He followed me out of the kitchen into the hallway and quietly said "Miss Crozier, I want to see you". Oh crap, I thought, and trailed behind him into the library, where he told me he didn't need me to contradict him, that I should just say yes sir and no sir. Then, to my complete amazement, he said "didn't you know the cook and the houseman had planned to have the extra helpings of fish for themselves?".

I couldn't believe my ears. He had just shown me again the low opinion and lack of respect he had for all of his domestic help. I wondered if he thought the same about me. He treated his servants like dirt. I thought, they shouldn't send convicts to prison — they should send them to work for Cooke.

CHAPTER 47

Beware: juvenile delinquent at work

On Monday night, on my way home from work, something felt wrong with my car, so I pulled over to the side of the busy highway and saw that one of the tires was almost flat. Thank goodness there was enough air left to make it to the closest service station. After a quick inspection, I was told there was nothing wrong with the tire but that someone had let the air out. I was surprised at this because I worked in a safe and secure neighborhood. Then, while the tire was being refilled, I took a closer look at my car and noticed a long, deep, scratch across the right rear passenger door, to the back of the car. In addition to the flat tire, my car had been "keyed".

I felt sick. Deep down, I knew that Mrs. Cooke's younger son had done it to get revenge. A week ago, he had caught hell from Mr. Cooke for the graffiti he had done around Marbella. I had discovered the graffiti earlier and pointed it out to Mr. Cooke. One of the graffiti spots was right smack in the middle of the door to the library.

Next morning, I told Mr. Cooke what had happened and who I thought was responsible. This took a lot of nerve on my part because I knew Mr. Cooke really liked the kid, but this time he had gone too far. Mr. Cooke listened to me very quietly and then asked me why I thought it was Mrs. Cooke's younger son. I told him it was just a gut feeling that I thought he was upset with me for showing the graffiti to him. I also told Mr. Cooke I knew what the boy had done with the oranges to the houseman's car (I didn't mention the severed brake line).

After thinking about what I had said, Mr. Cooke told me he agreed with me, that he also thought the boy was responsible for a lot of the vandalism going on around Marbella. He told me he wanted me (not him!) to tell all of this to Mrs. Cooke later that day when she joined him in the library. Oh great, I thought, nothing like jumping from the frying pan into the fire.

Later that afternoon after Mr. and Mrs. Cooke had poured their pre-dinner glasses of wine, I came into the library and told Mrs. Cooke what had happened. Mr. Cooke acted as if he was hearing my story for the first time and asked me why I thought it was Mrs. Cooke's son. After I finished, Mr. Cooke called the boy into the library and questioned him and, just as I expected, he denied everything. Because it was I – and not Mr. Cooke – who had reported the incident to his mother, the boy saw me as the bad guy for the second time. Mr. Cooke had expertly trapped me again and I wondered what would happen to my car next.

Mr. Cooke told me he felt badly about my car and half-heartedly apologized and offered to pay for the damage. I thanked him and told him I wasn't going to have it repainted because it was an old car and I didn't have another car to use while it was in the shop. I thought he might take the hint and offer to lend me one of his cars but he didn't, so the damage was never fixed.

The big shindig at Potomac Yard was the next day and Mr. Cooke could barely contain his excitement. The press was once again gathered outside Marbella's gates. The ninth draft of Mr. Cooke's speech had been prepared and his friend and neighbor, playwright Larry King, put the finishing touches on it.

CHAPTER 48

Press conference day

The big day had finally arrived and there was excitement in the air. On my way to Marbella, I heard some guy on the radio talk about the INS starting deportation proceedings against Mrs. Cooke. Wow. Today was supposed to be Mr. Cooke's big day and already someone was trying to put a big stain on it.

The second I arrived at Marbella, I was greeted by an unhappy cook who told me he was upset with me for telling Mr. Cooke about the address cards missing from the rolodex on my desk and about the cook overhearing Mrs. Cooke's younger son telling a friend about it on the phone. (Earlier, when I had mentioned the missing cards to the cook, he told me what he had seen and heard.) Apparently, last night, Mr. Cooke jumped all over the cook for telling me about it and accused him of being an "informant and a narc". Major drama! And there I was, caught in the middle again! I thought that by telling Mr. Cooke about it, it would only offer further proof that the boy was up to more mischief. I didn't understand why Mr. Cooke would turn it around and jump all over his cook. Mr. Cooke had been looking for proof of the boy's bad behavior and when he finally got it he didn't like it.

Mr. Cooke was very edgy this morning and I figured it was just last minute jitters before the press conference. I went to the kitchen (my forbidden place) to get a fresh cup of coffee and came right back to my office. I had been away from my desk for only a minute. I found Mr. Cooke standing next to his desk with a panicked look on his face, saying he thought he was all alone, that he couldn't find me. I explained where I had been and he said “well, have him (the cook) do it. I need you here”. That was why I never took lunches or breaks; he could never understand why I wasn’t at his beck and call every single minute of the day. He even went crazy when I had to go to the bathroom. My office was my prison every day from the time I arrived until the time I left.

As lunch time grew closer, the rhythm of Marbella changed and everything became focused on the press conference. Mr. & Mrs. Cooke disappeared into their respective dressing rooms where they had their lunch and got themselves all gussied up and ready to leave for Potomac Yard. The houseman applied last minute spit and shine to the limo. I was in constant contact with staff from Kent Farms and Redskin Park. All the pieces were moving into place and all the players preparing to take the stage.

At the appointed time, Mr. & Mrs. Cooke emerged, both dressed to the nines: Mr. Cooke, the squire, in his trademark Hermes natty tweeds, complete with tweed hat; and Mrs. Cooke in her trademark Chanel couture, complete with Kentucky Derby style wide brimmed hat. What a curious couple they made, the 80+ year old “Billionaire Bully” and his 30 or 40-something year old “Bolivian Bombshell” wife.

I looked at her and thought “yeah baby, I know your deal; you’re the old guy’s paid arm candy”. I figured that once her job was done for today’s big show, it wouldn’t be long before she would disappear from Marbella again and not come back until either she needed something or Mr. Cooke baited her with another pricey piece of jewelry. Off they went in the limo. After they left, I scrambled around to get myself ready for the press conference. I was wearing Le Mart Du K and was driving myself in my – yup, still had it – ’74 Chevy Nova with the nice big scratch down the side.

The attendee list was a who’s who of local newscasters and sportscasters, Redskins, local politicians, and special guests. It was held under huge tents in the middle of the vacant tract of land in Alexandria, VA called Potomac Yard, where Mr. Cooke expected to build his new stadium. Every minute of the event had been precisely choreographed and it went off without a hitch, a complete success. Nothing dared go wrong. Even Mrs. Cooke's performance was worthy of an Oscar; she played her part perfectly, gazing upon Mr. Cooke with adoring eyes the entire time, giving everyone the impression they were the perfect couple. It was a very triumphant and proud moment for Mr. Cooke.

After a couple of hours, it was all over. Back to Marbella we all went. Mr. Cooke was a total pleasure to be around for the rest of the afternoon, as he basked in all the attention and watched himself on all the news broadcasts. It had been a long and exhausting day and I was thankful to finally get home and throw on some shorts and a t-shirt.

CHAPTER 49

Matters of the heart

During the week following the press conference, things started out pretty smooth but as the week went on, the calm pace at Marbella soon turned into a runaway train. I secretly got a little bit of personal satisfaction when I heard Mr. Cooke call his secretary at Kent Farms a "dope" over the phone. Mrs. Cooke and her younger son had taken off for their vacation in Hawaii and Mr. Cooke threw himself into his work with a vengeance. My office became a war zone. I was drowning in paper and there was no relief in sight.

After Mrs. Cooke had been in Hawaii for a while, Mr. Cooke received a letter from an older woman protesting the Redskins leaving Washington and going to Virginia. Surprisingly, he took heart to this "dear woman" and dictated his heart out to her — pages and pages! I couldn't believe it. It seemed that he was so lonely he would to talk to anyone.

On July 21, after spending a couple of days in Los Angeles on her way home from Hawaii, Mrs. Cooke called from LAX to tell Mr. Cooke she had missed her plane (gee, why was I not surprised?) even though she had been delivered right to the terminal in plenty of time by one of Mr. Cooke's LA staff. Mr. Cooke was bitterly disappointed at her irresponsibility. He had really missed her and had been counting the hours until her plane would touch down at Dulles. He kept asking me, and everyone else he spoke to, if we had ever missed a plane. And then he'd say he had never missed a plane. He said he should have had the driver handcuff himself to Mrs. Cooke and physically put her on the plane. Then he went on and on, saying "she is nothing but a 'star boarder' at Marbella" and that she "carries no weight and no responsibilities". I thought "Hallelujah! Now you're getting it, aren't you?"

Mr. Cooke was finally getting fed up with dealing with all of Mrs. Cooke's problems: the deportation proceedings, her older son's education problems, her younger son's budding career with vandalism, et cetera. He was preaching to the choir! I couldn't believe he was just now beginning to get the real picture. It was a full-time job dealing with all of Mrs. Cooke's and her sons' issues and needs. What really frustrated the heck out of me was her apathetic attitude towards everything (except shopping). Mr. Cooke (and his unfortunate staff) ended up taking care of everything while Mrs. Cooke just went shopping, took trips and ran away from home.

Yesterday was the younger son's 13th birthday – a big birthday for anyone — and Mr. Cooke wanted to have a party. He and I took care of all the planning and decorating. Mrs. Cooke didn't get involved until the last minute. Once the party began, she was attentive to her son and they appeared to have a good time, although, to me, it seemed more like "you WILL have fun".

There was a poolside barbecue with the cook grilling the burgers and hotdogs and the houseman serving, and Mr. & Mrs. Cooke taking the obligatory photos. Sort of a June, Ward, Wally and the Beave moment — Billionaire style. Mrs. Cooke's mother was also there. I was also asked (actually, more like *told*) by Mr. Cooke to join them for the barbecue. I took a seat off to the side of the table, ate my hot dog, smiled and laughed at the right times and waited for my enforced fun to come to an end.

Later, after the birthday party broke up and Mrs. Cooke was in the library with Mr. Cooke and her mother, they began discussing the deportation proceedings against Mrs. Cooke because her mother needed to complete some forms connected with the case. Suddenly, Mrs. Cooke went crazy and started yelling at her mother, shouting such awful things to her that Mr. Cooke, in his loud, booming voice, ordered her out of the library and then locked the door behind her. What a scene!

The next thing I knew, Mr. Cooke called me into the library and asked me what I thought of Mrs. Cooke's behavior. I had learned from past experience that I had to tread these waters very carefully. I needed time to think! I shook my head and said I couldn't understand it, that there was obviously a lot of anger there, that I could never talk to my mother that way because she was my best friend. I did not want to be in there. I desperately wanted to be dismissed so I could go hide in my office.

Unfortunately, Mr. Cooke went on, saying he was really getting fed up, that dealing with all this nonsense was taking a toll and that Mrs. Cooke wasn't any good for him. He told me his closest advisors were telling him to get rid of her. He said he thought he agreed, that he needed a wife (ye gods, I thought, another one?!) who was more of an asset, who was more socially inclined and who would run his house for him. (And I thought "Duh, hello? What exactly did you expect when you married the Bolivian Bombshell?!") Later that afternoon, Mrs. Cooke predictably left Marbella and returned to her apartment in Alexandria.

CHAPTER 50

"Did you hear that Miss Crozier?"

Abandoned by his wife once again, Mr. Cooke stayed in bed and read his newspapers and sipped his tea. He was in a very reflective and contemplative mood. When I took his papers in to him, he looked up at me and quietly said "what a life I have eh?". I agreed with him and told him it was not an easy one in spite of what others might think. What I really wanted to say was "you made your bed and now you're lying in it". He dismissed me and I returned to my office.

After a couple of hours, Mr. Cooke came into the library and sat at his desk. It wasn't long before the day started to go downhill and the drama started up again. Mrs. Cooke came briefly to Marbella to look in on her older son who had had plastic surgery on his nose. The second I saw her enter the library, I rushed to my door and closed it. I knew there was going to be trouble. The vocal crescendo began to build and soon became an all out shouting match. Seated at my desk, my head in my hands and my eyes closed, I willed the argument to stop.

Suddenly and without warning, Mr. Cooke called me in there and had me stand between him and Mrs. Cooke. There was no way I wanted to be in there. Mrs. Cooke was sitting in the chair to the side of the desk, clutching her 350 page deportation proceeding transcript to her chest, both her arms folded around it, and struggling to keep her husband from taking it from her. He was playfully swiping at it, trying to take it, but she kept moving her arm around and I was afraid she would reinjure her recently gunshot finger. She was saying "you will hurt my finger, Jack" and he kept saying "I'm not hurting her finger, am I, Miss Crozier"? Then he asked me "Am I harassing her, Miss Crozier?"

Oh my God, I thought, this can't possibly be happening. As diplomatically as I could, I shakily replied "I don't know, Mr. Cooke, I haven't seen anything until now".

Then, as he stepped away from Mrs. Cooke and the shouting continued, he turned to me and clearly said "Miss Crozier, I want you to stand right there and witness everything that is being said". I was mortified; I wanted to die. Before I could react or do anything, the argument spun out of control. She screamed at him "you are a son of a bitch; you are a fucking son of a bitch and I hate you; I hate you more than The Bitch hates you!". Then she said "you are a bully; no wonder The Bitch hated you so much". Then he turned to me and said "Did you hear all that, Miss C?" I was dying inside. I whimpered "yes sir". And then she stepped right in front of me and shouted "Did you hear that Miss Crozier? I'll repeat it for you." And, after shouting the hateful words again, she fled from the library.

All the time I was in the library I tried to make myself as small as possible. I wanted to dig a hole and crawl into it and curl up in a fetal position. I wanted to disappear. I knew Mr. Cooke was my employer and that I should be loyal to him, but everything had sunk to a whole new level. I felt very strongly that I did not belong in that room in the middle of such a fierce battle between a husband and wife. I wondered if there was nothing that was private or sacred to the man.

I was thankful it was Friday afternoon. I couldn't wait to get away from Marbella and all the insanity.

CHAPTER 51

Just knock on the door

One morning, shortly after I arrived, Mr. Cooke called me from his bathroom phone and told me to be sure to knock on the bathroom door when a certain person called him. When the call came through, I walked through Mr. Cooke's bedroom (after first knocking), to his bathroom and knocked on the door as I was told to do. What I didn't expect was that he would open the door and be standing there totally naked with shaving cream on his face. Yikes!!! Thanks for that lovely vision Mr. Cooke! I'll sleep real well tonight! I looked away as quickly as I could and, without missing a beat, he asked me what I wanted. Keeping my eyes averted, I told him the call he wanted was holding and, without waiting to be dismissed, high-tailed it out of there.

It took me a while to recover from that little episode. He obviously had no respect for me – none! And what was worse, I was sure he got a laugh out of terrorizing his poor secretary.

CHAPTER 52

Northern Lights, loons and moose

Somehow I found the strength to survive the last week and made it to a much needed week of vacation which I had planned with my college friend and fellow nature lover, Sally. Our plan was to drive to the tip of Michigan's Upper Peninsula and take a boat to the remote and wild Isle Royale in Lake Superior where we would spend several days hiking, observing loons, moose and, with a little luck, wolves.

On Friday, I left work at 1:30 to catch my flight out of Dulles. I should have known right from the start there would be problems. First, the taxi couldn't find my apartment and as a result I arrived at Dulles just 30 minutes before my flight and had to run like hell through the busy airport to get to my gate. Then a storm blew through which caused huge delays. Five hours later, my flight finally departed for Detroit. Sally greeted me at the airport and we drove to her home in Ann Arbor where her twin sister, Susie, was waiting with celebratory wine and munchies.

We had a lot of catching up to do and we partied almost all night. At about 4:00 am, Sally and I started loading up her Bronco for the long trip up the UP. Somehow, during all our running back and forth with our bags between the house and the Bronco, we discovered my backpack and a couple of jackets were missing. We looked everywhere. They were gone! Sally told me there were some homeless folks in the area and that they had probably been snatched up by one of them. How ironic I thought, nothing is safe anymore, not even at 4 am. I was really bummed because my backpack had all my "good stuff" in it: jewelry, toiletries, new swimsuit, favorite jeans etc. Before we turned in, we made sure the rest of our things were securely packed and locked inside the Bronco.

After three hours of alcohol-induced sleep, we left Ann Arbor for Sally's parents' home in Adrian for a picnic with the entire family (12 brothers & sisters!), most of whom I had come to know over the years. It was a gorgeous summer afternoon and we had the barbecue in the huge, freshly mown backyard, surrounded by woods. At about 7:30 pm, stuffed on burgers, hotdogs and potato salad, Sally and I hit the road for our big adventure. We drove until 2:30 am, stopped for a few hours of sleep, and then made the rest of the drive to Copper Harbor, where, the next morning, we would catch the boat for Isle Royale.

We took our time and stopped and picnicked along the way. There were so many beautiful places to see it was amazing we made any headway. We could have spent the entire week just exploring the UP. In Copper Harbor, we stayed up half the night hoping to see the Northern Lights, but we had no luck. At 8 o'clock the next morning we left by boat for Isle Royale.

Four and a half hours later the boat docked at Isle Royale in a chilly, driving rain, but breaks in the clouds gave us hope that the weather would soon clear. And oh man did it ever! By 4 o'clock the sky was bright blue and the air was crisp. It couldn't get any better than that. We had an early dinner so we could get in a quick four mile hike before we lost daylight. There were Loons everywhere! They were all over the place, flying, swimming and dozing lazily on the water while they gently rocked back and forth on the sunlit ripples. And their voices! Long, haunting calls and yodels . . . they were indescribably wonderful! That night we stayed up late again looking for the Northern Lights but they still eluded us.

A 10 mile hike was on our agenda for the next morning. We took picnic lunches with us which had been prepared by the dining room staff. It was a picture perfect day. While walking on a boardwalk through a bog, I took my eyes off of where I was walking and took a tumble onto my left hand, bending my fingers back. Ouch! A quick lesson learned to always keep your eyes in front of you! We continued our hike, eager to see our first moose.

Shortly after we started our return to the lodge, a hiker heading in the opposite direction excitedly told us that he had seen three moose cows swimming at the lower end of Tobin Bay! We were still about a mile and a half from there, so we double timed it. As we approached the bay, we began to hear unmistakable moose sounds and, as the water came into view, we were rewarded with the sight of our first moose – two cows, both in the water. Careful not to make any noise, we sat and silently watched and listened for about 15 minutes. Nature at its finest!

We returned to camp at about 3 pm and, completely exhausted, I fell onto my bed and was sound asleep within minutes. After a couple of hours, I got up to go to dinner with Sally and afterwards, still tired, I went back to bed. At around 3 am, Sally woke me up and told me the Northern Lights were putting on a show. So, out into the night we both went to watch the amazing solar display.

We arose early the next morning and, after quick breakfast, we went canoeing – seven hours of it, and on a windy day, no less. That little canoe outing of ours ended up being more comical than anything. What a pair we made: me with my phobia of seeing rocks in the water and Sally with her prosthetic arm (she had lost her right arm in a car accident during high school). Determined, we got into our canoe and pushed off from the shore. Right away, the wind started blowing us around all over the place. While Sally struggled to get a rhythm with her paddle and to keep it from popping out of her prosthetic hand over and over again, I was squealing and panicking at every rock I saw. I kept my eyes focused on the tree tops and sky and not down at the scary rocks and just paddled like crazy. Miraculously, we made it to a tiny island that had a small sandy beach.

Exhausted, and realizing we were totally out of our element and had bitten off more than we could chew, we scrambled out of the canoe onto the island and sat on a tree that had fallen over. We were both speechless and we waited for our heart rates to return to normal. After a few minutes, we apologized for the comments we had made to each other during our mutual panic attacks. Before we knew it, we started to laugh and soon we were laughing so hard we were almost peeing ourselves. Not quite ready to get back into the canoe yet, we just sat there and took in the peace of the island and watched for wildlife. We were soon rewarded with the site of a young bull moose which slowly emerged from the thick undergrowth of the shoreline to step down to the water for a drink.

Well, it was time to get back in the canoe. We had to do it sooner or later. We looked at each other and, saying "here goes nothing", got back into the canoe for our scary paddle back to the other shore. In spite of my shrieks at rocks and Sally's one-handed paddling and the wind constantly testing us, we finally made it back, our friendship still intact.

After we returned to camp, I checked out the gift shop and Sally went to our room. While paying for some postcards, I heard someone shout "moose!". I dropped everything and ran to the door. There was a young bull moose that had come down from the woods, through the little village and down to the water. Everybody went crazy! The lucky ones – me included — had their cameras. Click, click, click went the shutters. After about 5 minutes, the moose decided he had had enough and disappeared back into the woods.

That evening, Sally went off with new acquaintances for more canoeing (she was determined to get it right!) and I, having had my fill of sunken rocks, went for a three mile hike.

The next day, our final day on the island, we got up early so we would have time to pack, check out, and go for a nice 4.5 mile hike before lunch and the long boat ride back to Copper Harbor. It was hard to leave such a beautiful and wild place. It had given me a sorely needed respite and total escape from all the madness that awaited me back home.

The boat arrived at Copper Harbor at 8 pm and we soon discovered the battery in Sally's Bronco needed a jump. After we were rescued by the boat captain's mate, we started our way back south, away from Lake Superior and down the length of the Upper Peninsula. We drove until about 1 am, stopped for some much needed sleep, and hit the road again at 7:30.

Sally was a hard core Dan Fogelberg fan and had gotten us tickets for his concert in Detroit that evening and there was no way we were going to miss that! It would be the perfect ending to our great adventure. But it meant we had to cover an awful lot of miles. After driving the entire length of the UP, we still had to drive down the entire length of Michigan to Detroit. It seemed like we drove forever. But we did it. Just minutes before the concert started, we pulled into the parking lot and dragged our tired butts to our seats. Fogelberg was fantastic and it was a miracle we were able to stay awake. After the concert, we still had 90 more miles to drive back to Ann Arbor. We both got so tired we had to spell each other every 10 minutes. We could barely keep our eyes open. Finally, the driving marathon came to an end and we pulled up to Sally's house. We left everything in the car and stumbled into the house. I was asleep before my head hit the pillow. The next day it was back to Virginia and reality.

CHAPTER 53

Welcome back from vacation

I had a bad case of the back-to-work blues. It was so hard to come back after the amazing vacation I had just had. I went from total escape and relaxation right back into the Jack Kent Cooke straight jacket. At about 9:30 last night, while I was savoring my last hours of freedom and lost in the magical memories of Isle Royale, Mr. Cooke called me to rag on me about a memo he thought I had done several weeks ago about Mrs. Cooke's younger son's tutoring schedule at St Albans. I tried to explain to him that the memo had actually been prepared by one of his secretaries from Kent Farms, but he didn't want to hear that. So I let him read me the riot act for 10 minutes because I knew that, afterwards, he would be fine and leave me alone for the rest of the evening. Yup, I was definitely back.

CHAPTER 54

A little bit of this, a little bit of that

A few days after my return from Michigan, I was working in my office while Mr. Cooke read his newspapers in the library. Apparently, he was unhappy with an article that had appeared in the Washington Post. He asked me to come into the library. He looked at me for a few seconds and then asked me what I had said to a reporter when they had called yesterday afternoon. Knowing he was looking for a way to blame me for the offending article, I looked right at him and replied "I told the reporter you weren't at home and we spoke of nothing else". If I had learned nothing else while working for Mr. Cooke, I learned DO NOT TALK TO REPORTERS!

This afternoon, while he was sipping wine with Mrs. Cooke in the library, Mr. Cooke quietly asked me to open his safe and bring him the $40,000 pair of Tiffany's custom-made ruby and diamond Redskin themed earrings. After I retrieved the earrings and gave them to him, he presented them to Mrs. Cooke who had just returned to Marbella after a 10 day absence. He just sat there, giddy with joy, and exclaimed to her over and over again "I love you, I love you".

I wanted to throw up. I didn't understand why he couldn't see through the game she played with him. It was simple, Naughty Wife 101: she'd run away from home; he'd plead for her to come back; she'd come back and he'd give her a big expensive reward. Here's your reward for coming home to papa. She was obviously milking him for everything she could get. I guessed that within one week the process would repeat itself all over again. I didn't feel sorry for him; he had created the monster.

Earlier today, the houseman came to me and reported there was a man sitting in his car watching the comings and goings at Marbella. He said the housekeeper told him she thought he had binoculars. I got a description of the man's car and the license plate numbers and then told Mr. Cooke about it. Without any hesitation, he got Coco's (his Cocker Spaniel) leash and walked her right up to the man's car and, in a friendly manner, asked the man who he was and where he worked and for how long he had worked. He found out the man was a cook at the nearby Omni Shoreham Hotel. He had arrived early for work and was waiting for a parking space to open up. False alarm!

CHAPTER 55

I could almost learn to like the guy

It had been a very quiet morning at Marbella and Mr. Cooke did not come into the library until almost noon. He was in a rare, peaceful frame of mind and, when I greeted him, he said "we slept in this morning; she's so nice when she wants to be". I was glad to hear Mrs. Cooke was still there and I told him so. He responded "we'll see how long it lasts" and I replied "well, enjoy it while it lasts" and he agreed that was not bad advice.

Mr. & Mrs. Cooke had breakfast at 1:30 and Mr. Cooke got a kick out of that and said "it's outrageous". He was in good spirits all day and even took Mrs. Cooke to a matinee which starred Clint Eastwood, before which he remarked "he's a good friend of mind you know". I really was happy for him and wished his life could be this peaceful all the time. God only knew, it sure would have made my life easier. I knew it wouldn't last though.

Later that day, I received the following memo from one of the secretaries at Kent Farms:

"When making reservations at Duke's for Mr. Cooke, never make the reservation through Betty. We are to speak to Duke or Randy, or whatever man is next in charge. Again, never make the reservation through Betty. Many thanks for your attention to this."

The memo was obviously the result of the recent fiasco at Duke's when his table had been given away — even though I had called ahead and informed the hostess (and, God forbid, not a man). She had committed the unforgiveable sin of not reserving Mr. Cooke's usual table and, as a result, ALL women were now considered incompetent!

CHAPTER 56

Tutoring and personal service

During the afternoon, Mr. Cooke asked me to come into the library and witness a conversation between him and Mrs. Cooke's older son regarding tutoring and his future. Here we go again, I thought, as I joined them. During the one-sided conversation, the boy understandably remained passive. I empathized with him, knowing that his life at Marbella wasn't easy. Mr. Cooke was so forceful and never missed an opportunity to remind everyone that it was HIS house and there was only one way to do things: HIS way.

Today, though, Mr. Cooke was offering the kid a great opportunity: free education. Burdened with my own college loans, I couldn't believe it when the boy responded that he wasn't interested. Only because Mr. Cooke had encouraged me to join in on the discussion, I told the boy that, years from now, he would be very sorry he didn't accept Mr. Cooke's generous offer. I told him that, contrary to what he thought (he was convinced he was stupid), he was not stupid – he was just uneducated, that everyone comes into this world uneducated — but not stupid — and that the two were very different from each other. After that, I was dismissed from the library. I never did find out if the boy accepted Mr. Cooke's offer.

The next day, Mr. Cooke was upset by the manager of the neighboring Omni Shoreham Hotel and his failure to personally handle Mr. Cooke's grandson's check-out, which resulted in his grandson being charged instead of Mr. Cooke, as previously arranged. He personally spoke with the manager and expressed his disappointment and, within an hour, a letter of apology and a gigantic basket full of goodies was delivered to Mr. Cooke, as well as a note saying there would be no charge for the room. I wondered if they would have done the same thing for Joe Blow?

CHAPTER 57

Christmas in August

When I arrived at Marbella this morning, Mr. Cooke greeted me and, out of the clear blue, told me my office was being moved to the Redskins new training facility and that I would be working there from now on. Hallelujah! I couldn't believe my ears! This was the best news ever! I felt like I was being released from prison. I knew that construction of a new Redskin Park had just been completed but never dared hope I would work there. And the icing on the cake was that I lived only a few miles away from the facility! I wouldn't have that nasty commute anymore! Mr. Cooke grabbed his briefcase and asked "Well, are you ready to go?". I was unprepared and surprised by the move and I still had to pack up my office, so I asked him if I could follow in a little bit and he was fine with that.

An hour and a half later, I arrived at Redskin Park, my car packed to the brim with boxes, typewriter, files, etc. The new facility was state of the art and it was beautiful. The interior was decorated in the Redskins trademark burgundy. The entry area was very spacious and there were showcases on one wall in which resided the Redskins' three Super Bowl trophies and countless other trophies and awards. On the walls were historical photographs of all the teams, coaches and star players. The place was a football fan's dream! There was an elevator that ran between the reception area and the lower level for hurt players and others unable to use the stairs. There was a wing for all the coaches' offices and a wing for the "front office" staff and the executive offices. The lower level was for the players: an impressive weight room, the locker room, a treatment room and even a basketball court. Outside, behind the building were four football fields with different surfaces. Mr. Cooke had built his world champion Redskins a palace.

Mr. Cooke's office was huge and occupied the corner of the executive wing, overlooking the practice fields. It had a wet bar and private bathroom. Our offices were connected and my office was very small, an anteroom to his office.

My first few days there were chaotic; at times there were four or five different types of construction people, technicians, etc in our offices, hooking up phones, fax machines, copy machines, computers (hooray, a computer!), and all the other latest technology.

I was so happy to be there! It was like a miracle had happened. I was now only a 10 minute drive from home, plus I wouldn't be caught in the middle of all the drama and problems at Marbella.

Redskin Park provided a "normal" working environment and I was surrounded by friendly faces. It got better each day as my office became more organized and the workmen and technicians gradually disappeared. My hours were changed to 9-5, which I loved. I even came in on the weekends for a few hours to get caught up since it was impossible to get any work done when Mr. Cooke was there because all he would do was interrupt, me constantly and, before I knew it, I had twenty different "right away" projects in process.

A few days after my move to the Park, I needed to call the cook at Marbella about something. When he answered the phone, I said "hi, (xxx), how are you?", before I got down to business. Big mistake! Mr. Cooke overheard me and came into my office and read me the riot act, saying "IT IS A TOTAL WASTE OF TIME, THAT PEOPLE DON'T REALLY CARE HOW PEOPLE ARE WHEN THEY ASK THAT QUESTION". Then he asked me if I knew how he handled his calls. I said "yes sir, you are very abrupt on the phone, sir".

(Well heck, it was true — he hung up on everyone, cut off conversations, and many times people had to call him back to finish what they were saying!)

During the next few days, I met a lot of the players and coaches. Every time I went to the kitchen, I was surrounded by players. Oh man, those guys loved to eat! If it was in the kitchen and wasn't moving, it got eaten. I had come to know Super Bowl MVP Mark Rypien, Charles Mann, Art Monk, Darrell Green, Jeff Bostic, Joe Jacoby, Jim Lachey and countless others. I also became friends with head coach Joe Gibbs, special teams coach Wayne Sevier (his wife, Barbara, was Joe Gibbs' secretary), General Manager Charley Casserly and all the front office staff. It was so nice to be around normal, friendly people!

I saw Mr. Cooke become a different person when he was at Redskin Park. He was at his best when he was wearing his "team owner hat". There was no doubt about it, he loved his Redskins.

Earlier, I had walked out into the parking lot with Charles Mann and told him we had just finished furnishing Mr. Cooke's office and that he should come by and take a look. So, I was not surprised when he appeared in my doorway and called out to me in that soft voice of his "show me that office". Mr. Cooke wasn't there, so I gave Charles the grand tour of the opulent office which was now filled with priceless antiques. It was the ultimate power office.

Now that I worked at Redskin Park and didn't have to commute to DC, I had a new life after 5 pm. Most days I rode my bicycle and other days I rode horses with friends. Life was good!

CHAPTER 58

NEVER DO THAT AGAIN, YOU SHOULD KNOW BETTER!

Mr. Cooke had finally approved three days of vacation for his cook. The poor guy really wanted a week but was afraid to ask for that much. I helped him out by typing up a nice memo to Mr. Cooke, asking for the three days and a quick answer so he could make his plans. Mr. Cooke approved the request, but also told the cook he was doing him a "big favor" by letting him take the days. What? A big favor for letting him take vacation time he had earned? Yowza! For the past 13 months, the cook had faithfully worked six days a week and had only missed one and a half days. I thought "wow, Mr. Cooke still thinks it's the mid 1800s and he's the 'Massa' and he owns the cook and the houseman!".

Yesterday, September 1, Mr. Cooke showed up at Redskin Park about noon and, right away, I noticed he was acting a little bit "off" and that his speech was slurred. I couldn't smell any alcohol on his breath and was concerned. Earlier, at his request, I had set on his desk 100 "compliments of Jack Kent Cooke" cards for him to sign, to be sent out with the new Redskins Yearbooks and Press Guides to his personal friends. He looked at the cards and, clearly puzzled, asked me why they were on his desk. After I explained, he told me the cards cost $.75 each and that if he were me he would use the less expensive "compliments of Washington Redskins" cards. Okay, I thought, the man has the right to change his mind, even though he had specifically told me he wanted to use the "good" cards.

Mr. Cooke was soon joined by his in-house counsel and Mr. John, and they stayed with him in his office for an hour or so, until he told me he wasn't feeling well and that he was going home. He really wasn't well and I was glad he was leaving and that his counsel had agreed to drive him, even though it meant he would have to leave his car at Redskin Park and wait at Marbella until his wife could pick him up. I later learned from the cook that, after they had arrived at Marbella, Mr. Cooke got nasty and turned on the houseman and his good samaritan. The cook also told me that when he asked Mr. Cooke if he should give dinner to general counsel, who was still waiting to be picked up, Mr. Cooke angrily replied, in front everyone, "I'm not going to ask him to sit at our table for dinner!". No good deed goes unpunished.

A Kent Farms staffer later told me that if Mr. Cooke ever became physically disabled, to look out because he would become insufferable. I couldn't imagine him being any worse and I hoped for everyone's sake that, when and if that time came, I would be long gone from there.

As the week went on, Mr. Cooke was still not feeling well and was lashing out at everyone! When he got like that, I would do everything I could to avoid upsetting him. I stayed at my desk every possible minute except for when I needed to go down the hall to the bathroom. And even then, I would try to limit those visits, to the point that when I did have to go to the ladies' room, I really had to go! Of course, it never failed that Mr. Cooke would call me whenever I made my mad dash to the bathroom, resulting in several Redskin staffers frantically searching for me. Once, when I was on my way back from that forbidden place, I was frantically flagged down and told Mr. Cooke was trying to find me. I ran as fast as I could back to my desk to pick up the phone. He was absolutely flabbergasted and asked me where I had been. When I told him where I had been, he ordered me to "NEVER DO THAT AGAIN, YOU SHOULD KNOW BETTER!" What ...???? Never go to the bathroom again??? YES SIR MR. COOKE!

Knowing my bladder had a mind of its own and that it wouldn't take orders even from Mr. Cooke, I had to find some kind volunteer who would lay their life on the line and sit at my desk whenever I needed to go. Talk about demeaning. I felt like I had to beg permission and apologize every time I needed to go make my bladder gladder. This was never an easy thing because no one in their right mind would intentionally put themselves in my hot seat and risk an encounter with Mr. Cooke.

CHAPTER 59

Jewish expressions?

Once in a while, during NFL season, Mr. Cooke would ask me to send game tickets to friends. Earlier today, he asked me to send tickets for the upcoming Redskins v Dallas game (the hottest tickets in town) to one of his friends. I drafted up a quick note for him to sign that would be delivered along with the tickets. At the end of the note, I used one of my favorite expressions, "Enjoy!", and took it in to him for signature. I stood by his desk while he scanned the note. Suddenly he looked up at me and exclaimed "NEVER use that expression -- don't you know 'enjoy' is a big Jewish expression?"

I cringed inwardly and didn't respond. I stole a peek at Mr. Cooke's architect (we had become friends and frequently commiserated about our run-ins with Mr. Cooke – the misery loves company sort of thing) who happened to be sitting at Mr. Cooke's desk to see what he thought of the prejudicial remark. I didn't really expect to see any reaction, though, because it was a good way to get one's self in trouble with Mr. Cooke.

CHAPTER 60

"You stay here now"

It wasn't long before Mr. Cooke called Redskin Park and asked me to come to Marbella. He was suffering an attack of shingles and gout, poor guy. He told me he didn't want to do any work; he just wanted me to watch the phones and sit with him because Mrs. Cooke "was not being much help".

Shortly after I arrived, he asked me to call his doctor to come to Marbella. The attentive doctor came right away. He examined Mr. Cooke and gave him some medicine to make him more comfortable. Mrs. Cooke had gone out and, unable to stay awake, he asked me to sit by his bedside, saying "I'm just going to take a nap now. You stay here. I don't want to be left alone". Then he turned onto his side and went to sleep.

I sat there glancing back and forth between the fire and Mr. Cooke. I wondered at the sight of the temporarily helpless man before me, and thought, there was the almighty and powerful Jack Kent Cooke, made so vulnerable by his pain and his years. As he peacefully dozed, momentarily relieved of his pain, he reminded me of a very young child who appears so angelic once he has fallen asleep and I knew that any second, without warning, the quiet interlude would come to an abrupt end, and the angel once again become the devil.

Evidently things were worse than ever between Mr. & Mrs. Cooke. The servants told me that Mrs. Cooke, her sons and her mother had all been living downstairs. Interestingly, after she returned to Marbella later in the day, Mrs. Cooke was uncharacteristically protective of Mr. Cooke, ordering the servants about and taking care of everything for Mr. Cooke. I had never before seen her so involved and it was nice to see for a change. I secretly wondered if she thought he was going to die and she wanted to make sure she stayed on his good side and in his will.

Mrs. Cooke's compassion was short-lived. Mr. Cooke spent the next day in bed and I happily remained at Redskin Park. We spoke only a couple of times during the day and again at 11 that night, when he called me at home, just wanting someone to talk to and not caring how late it was. He told me Mrs. Cooke had walked out in a huff after a big argument and that he was very tired. Then he asked me if he deserved to be treated like that. Oh crap, what was I supposed to say? And why was he calling me so late anyway?

I told him what he wanted to hear, that he had done an awful lot to help Mrs. Cooke and her boys and that he was really the one who held the family together. I really laid it on thick, hoping that would satisfy him and he'd hang up. He seemed to like what he heard and asked me if I would repeat it in court if it ever became necessary. Praying I would never have to do that, I said I would. Finally, he said "good night" and hung up.

CHAPTER 61

Overeaters Anonymous

There was food everywhere at Redskin Park! Unless I wanted to put on the "freshman 10" I was gonna have to be strong and ignore all the food that kept getting delivered for the players and staff by all the local restaurants. Every time I went in the kitchen I saw beautiful platters full of every kind of food you could imagine. Especially tempting were the incredible cakes delivered every Thursday by the Alpine Restaurant.

CHAPTER 62

The Medusa

Mr. Cooke had again decided to fire his cook. Like a cat playing with a mouse, he was really giving the cook a hard time before he finally fired him. This time, it was over the beer and wine inventory at Marbella. Mr. Cooke had personally kept track of the inventory for the past four months because someone was apparently helping his or herself. The missing beer was unaccounted for and, since neither he nor Mrs. Cooke drank beer and he was convinced that Mrs. Cooke's sons would never drink it (dream on!), the prime suspect was the big bad cook. The fact that the cook had freely admitted his love for beer had not helped matters and Mr. Cooke had made up his mind that the cook was guilty.

But there was more to this story. The cook told me that last Sunday night, when he went to his favorite jazz club in DC's Adams Morgan district, a popular nightclub spot, he saw Mrs. Cooke there, having dinner and holding hands with another man. Before he could get away, Mrs. Cooke saw him. He knew then and there that he was going to be fired. He had seen the same thing happen to a houseman. Mrs. Cooke had had the houseman quickly and neatly eliminated from the household. Now the same thing was happening to the cook. The writing was on the wall.

Getting back to the beer, the cook knew for a fact that the beer had been drunk by the houseman and Mrs. Cooke's older son and some of his friends. The beer had disappeared last weekend when the cook wasn't even there. But Mr. Cooke was still blaming him. He was paying the price for Mrs. Cooke's indiscretion. It wasn't fair and I hated seeing it happen. The only thing I could do for him was advise him to write a letter to Mr. Cooke and leave it on his way out. I told him the letter should be his final say and that it should clear him of all of Mr. Cooke's false accusations and set the record straight.

Before the cook left, he told me the houseman had recently found a bag of marijuana in Mrs. Cooke's older son's room and that he had told the houseman to report it right away to Mr. Cooke. For reasons unknown to me, he never reported it. Personally, I thought it would have been a perfect opportunity to get revenge after the kid had called him the "N word" to his face. The cook also told me the housekeeper kept finding empty beer bottles in the boy's bedroom. Geez, I thought, how lazy can you get? At least get rid of the evidence! Why Mr. Cooke chose to ignore the boys' bad behavior was beyond me. I guessed it was just easier to accuse the resident slaves.

Within a few days, both the cook and the houseman were gone. The cook called to say good bye and told me Mr. Cooke had given him $250 in severance pay. Geez, I hoped he wouldn't spend it all one place. Countless times Mr. Cooke had told me he trusted the cook with his life. He had been a faithful employee and had always gone the extra mile for Mr. Cooke. He had never complained and always answered "yes sir" with a smile on his face. I would miss him.

CHAPTER 63

"Oh boy aren't you something else"

The last couple of weeks were crazy. Mr. Cooke had been putting in long hours at Redskin Park and that made my life hell because when he was there I couldn't get anything done. Work piled up all over the place and, to make matters worse, I had computer problems. Also, Mr. Cooke still wasn't feeling all that great and that made him more irritable than usual (hmm, how would I have known the difference?).

A couple of days ago, two technicians were in my office trying to get my printer to work. Forgetting that they were actually there to help the situation, Mr. Cooke snuck up on them, scaring the hell out of them, and ordered them out of my office, exclaiming "WE'RE TRYING TO RUN A BUSINESS HERE! YOU HAVE JUST ABOUT RUINED MY WHOLE AFTERNOON! GET OUT!" The guys dropped their tools and ran for their lives. I could understand Mr. Cooke not wanting to have to deal with workmen in my office during working hours, but sometimes, there was nothing we could do about it, especially when it came to computers.

As luck would have it, about 15 minutes after Mr. Cooke left for home, Mrs. Cooke called for him. I dreaded it whenever she called because it always meant trouble. I knew that no matter how I handled her call or her message, Mr. Cooke would be frustrated and angry. Anything I did would be wrong. Resigned to that fact, I told her he was on his way home and gave her the number for the BMW (she was incapable of looking up a phone number, let alone memorizing it). Then I waited five minutes and called Mr. Cooke to tell him she had called and asked him if she had reached him in the BMW. He calmly said "no", but then suddenly launched into a tirade and said I "should have told her there was a good chance Mr. Cooke was on the phone but I would make sure he called her as soon as he was available. . . that I should have known he was on a very lengthy call with his counsel" and ended with "oh boy, aren't you something else". I had never seen anybody get so hyper-sensitive about phone calls from their wife! Instead of wasting his time and energy ranting at me all he had to do was pick up his phone and call her!

CHAPTER 64

Happy Birthday Cat

My birthday was yesterday. The night before, I was at the Redskins game until 1:30 am and I had to be at work early that morning to get everything ready for Mr. Cooke's meeting with Virginia's Governor. I had to do a lot of running around and because my desk had to be manned at all times, it was a logistical nightmare. As usual, before I could leave my desk, I had to first find some kind hearted soul who would be willing to sit in the hot seat and risk abuse a la Cooke. Most of the time, everything worked out ok, but there were times when I returned to my office after just a few minutes that I would find a wild eyed, panic stricken staffer wanting to bolt out of my office the second she saw me coming. I owed a lot of favors.

The meeting with the Governor took place in Mr. Cooke's office. It was an important meeting and concerned negotiations for the new Redskins stadium site. Mr. Cooke wanted to get his new stadium built. Time was growing short and the deal needed to be struck soon, plus it needed to be good enough to present to a special session of the Virginia State Legislature for approval. The Governor told Mr. Cooke they needed to come up with a plan by the end of the week. The pressure was on, Mr. Cooke was still not feeling well, and things were not looking good for the Potomac Yard deal. The meeting dragged on for what seemed like forever and then quietly ended. I had the impression that things hadn't gone well.

I thought about Monday night's nationally televised game and how exciting it was. The Redskins were amazing. They played with the same fire as when they had won last year's Super

Bowl. But it was Art Monk who stole the show when he broke the all-time receiving record. A spontaneous celebration broke out on the field and all the team members rushed to Art and hoisted him up on their shoulders. The crowd went nuts and the roar was deafening. I thought all the jumping up and down might bring down the old RFK Stadium. Oh man was I lucky to be a part of such an incredible organization!

After I moved to Redskin Park, I started making my special chocolate chip cookies for the team after every game. Today, I brought the cookies in and took them to the kitchen where I knew the guys would be coffeeing up for the team meeting. I proudly set them on the counter and announced "these cookies are for you because you're so great". Not known for shyness where food was concerned, they dove right in. Even Jim Lachey, who suffered a (career ending) injury to his knee in last night's game, was there and grabbed a few. After ten minutes, there was nothing left except a few crumbs.

Shortly after their meeting, Mr. Cooke and the Governor announced that their consideration of Potomac Yard as the site for the new Redskins stadium had been irrevocably withdrawn. That meant Mr. Cooke had to start all over again to find a place to build his new stadium. I honestly felt bad for him.

Later today, two days after my birthday, I called Mr. Cooke to tell him his new housekeeper had called from Chicago's O'Hare Airport, her long flight from the Philippines having just landed. Before I could finish the message, he cut me off and growled loudly "I could care less, just fax me the message" and hung up. I shook my head and thought "oh what a joyful creature you are Mr. Cooke". I felt bad for this new housekeeper who had traveled such a long way and had no idea what was in store for her. What a formidable slave master Mr. Cooke would have been during the 1800s in the land of Dixie.

CHAPTER 65

Happy Birthday Mr. Cooke

Mr. Cooke turned 80 yesterday. On Friday, he was full of anticipation for his birthday. His son from Kentucky, "Mr. Ralph", and his wife were flying in for the big event, so Mr. Cooke planned a festive family weekend. Also on Friday, Mr. Cooke sat alongside the practice field and watched the Redskins go through their drills. After the practice ended, all the players and coaches came over to him and sang "Happy Birthday", while the front office staff watched from the balcony. It was a very happy occasion and Mr. Cooke drank it all in.

I was relieved to hear that Mr. Cooke's special family weekend went smoothly and that there were no glitches. And as the celebratory weekend came to a close, the Redskins even managed to present Mr. Cooke with a birthday victory over the Minnesota Vikings. A perfect ending to a perfect weekend!

Today was a different ballgame, though, and, apparently having a case of the post-birthday blues, Mr. Cooke, who was still getting used to the new phone system at Redskin Park, buzzed me and asked me how to get an outside line and make a call. I started to answer "you dial . . ." and he cut me off in his usual impatient manner told me he didn't need me to tell him to dial, that I should just say the number. Ugh! Get yourself a robot Mr. Cooke!

Later on I had to rush off two sets of Mrs. Cooke's hand x-rays to a doctor in California. As usual, Mr. Cooke needed to be in control and he personally made all the phone calls and arrangements. He always gave me the impression that he was desperately afraid if he even slightly loosened his grip on her she would, like a captive bird, fly away from him as fast as she could. She had already proven that.

CHAPTER 66

Coach Joe Gibbs: class act

A couple of days ago, on Saturday, I brought my friends Hal, Sandy and John to Redskin Park and give them a tour. It was fun to see the now familiar Redskin Park through fresh eyes. Excitement and awe were written all over their faces when we came in the front door and entered the reception area where their eyes feasted on the three Super Bowl trophies and all the other memorabilia.

It was just after 6 pm, the day before the Redskins v Giants game. The team meeting had just ended and the players and coaches were getting ready to go out into the wet foggy night for a quick practice. One of the coaches came right up to Hal and John and introduced himself and offered to take them downstairs for a tour of the weight room, treatment room and locker room. They were thrilled to meet Super Bowl MVP Mark Rypien and Charles Mann before they came back upstairs.

Coach Gibbs' secretary, Barbara, gave us a tour of the coaches' wing, including Gibbs' office where his recently acquired Daytona 500 trophy was proudly displayed. While we stood outside of his office, an understandably distracted Joe Gibbs passed by and nodded a quick hello to me. I knew my friends were dying to meet him but I didn't want to interrupt his preparation for the next day's big game so I nodded back at him and didn't pursue an introduction for my friends.

Next, I took my friends down to the executive wing to show them Mr. Cooke's impressive office and my unimpressive office.

Unexpectedly, Coach Gibbs came around the corner and into my office and asked to meet my guests. I was so surprised that he had taken the time to make a special trip down to that end of the building so I could introduce him to my friends who, as well as I, felt extremely honored. What a class act!

I felt very proud to show Redskin Park to my friends. Without having to ask anyone or say a single word, we were extended every courtesy and treated with great respect and kindness.

CHAPTER 67

A red carpet day for my Dad

As it turned out, the Giants clobbered the Redskins. It was a horrible game in horrible weather. A miserable night all around. The next morning, with everyone feeling the loss, things were very quiet at Redskin Park. Mr. Cooke arrived and combined his "good morning" with "and wasn't it a horrible game last night" and then went right on with business as usual. In other words: IT (the game) was mentioned and should not be brought up again.

Mr. Cooke continued to poke and prod me as the somber day wore on. When he asked me about things I knew nothing about (to which I replied "I don't know sir"), he accused me of having no memory. When he read my note asking him if I could leave work at 1:30 on a Friday in November so I could get an early start on my drive up to New Jersey to visit my parents, he grumbled "yes, I suppose, but it seems like you're always doing something". Geez! I hardly EVER asked if I could leave work early! I couldn't let him get away with that remark so I said "No, I don't always have something going on" and asked if he was upset about my request, to which he responded that it was "just a passing remark, it's okay".

Later that day, my father, who had been in DC on business, stopped by the Park to say hello. I was really excited to show the place to Dad. And luckily, by then, Mr. Cooke's mood had greatly improved. For some reason, he decided to go all out for my Dad. He invited Dad into his office and had him sit down at his desk and shot the breeze with him for 20 minutes. And then he called the head PR guy and told him to take my father down to the field to watch the team practice. I couldn't believe it! What an amazing experience for my father! I was so happy for my Dad and so appreciative of Mr. Cooke's kindness to him. I knew that day would become a wonderful memory for both my Dad and me.

While Dad was down at the practice field, who should come walking down the hallway with Bobby Mitchell, but none other than Terry Bradshaw! I sprang up from my desk and ran out into the hallway and wouldn't let Bobby go any further without introducing me to the famous former Steeler quarterback. When Terry shook my hand, it completely disappeared. I had never before seen such huge hands. He was bigger than life and a real fun guy. We chatted for a few minutes and then he and Bobby went on their way.

What a day! I would never forget it. It gave me such an emotional high and made me appreciate the privileges and experiences I had that most people never even dream of. The outstanding events of this day helped give me the strength to push on and face all the obstacles that Mr. Cooke continued to toss in my way.

CHAPTER 68

Peaks and valleys

One afternoon, about a week after my father's visit, Mr. Cooke went from Dr. Jekyll to Mr. Hyde right before my eyes. He had been so pleasant most of the day, complimenting me on everything I did, and then, just like that, he became nasty, saying things like "I HAVE TO CLEAN UP LOOSE ENDS AFTER YOU ALL DAY LONG . . . BOY OH BOY YOU'RE REALLY SOMETHING . . . I LEAVE YOU ALONE FOR A FEW MINUTES AND EVERYTHING GOES TO HELL . . ."

Later, Mr. John came to his father's office and stayed there for over an hour. I hated it whenever they were there together because they would act like a couple of immature 12 year old boys with a secret language all their own. Mr. Cooke needed to dictate a couple of letters, so I went in and sat at his desk. Mr. John was seated on one of the sofas. Within minutes they started trading sarcastic wisecracks about staff members or other innocent people and rolling their eyes, making me feel like a fool. All I could do was answer back "yes sir" while, together, they would laugh at their secret little jokes.

At the end of the day, Mr. Cooke and Mr. John were driving back to DC together when Mr. Cooke called and started giving me hell. He had made up new rules again and everything was wrong. He was angry because I didn't have Mr. John and his LA man's names on the distribution list for his itinerary for his trip to Kentucky the next day. (Hello! Mr. Cooke! You reviewed and approved it, and let me remind you that you had never wanted anyone – including your sons and your LA guy –

to know what your business was!) Oh well, I guessed it was my fault for not getting out my crystal ball and reading his mind. Now he wanted everyone to know everything! I knew that if I had included the names in the distribution, he would have looked at me and said "what in the hell did you put their names on here for? They don't need to know what I'm doing". I couldn't win.

And if that wasn't enough, he ranted at me because his man in LA told him someone from the Kent Farms office was faxing messages to his home instead of his office. Of course, I knew nothing about that, but he didn't care.

By now I had been the target for Mr. Cooke's attacks so often that, believe it or not, I was actually developing a knack to tune it all out and just robotically utter the required responses, "yes sir" or "no sir", at the right times. I was learning to survive and my skin was growing thicker.

With this job came big highs and lows and when Mr. Cooke did a number on you, he took you from the top of Mt Everest and, by the throat, plunged you down into the depths of hell. He did it so well and so fast it left you sitting there in a heap, wondering "what the heck just happened?". She's up! She's down! She's up! She's down! People must have thought I was a real psycho.

Someone came up with a great analogy for Mr. Cooke and I couldn't have said it any better: "He steps on gnats and lets elephants run by".

OK, so before I could recover from that nasty little chew-out, I got shot out of a cannon right back to the top of Mt Everest! I was working away at my desk and something made me look up. I almost fell off my chair when I saw, standing in my doorway, actor Rodney Grant who played the fierce Native American warrior, "Wind in His Hair", in the film "*Dances With Wolves*". I was reduced to a puddle of goo. I had fallen in love with him when I saw the film and now there he was standing there in my office, with that beautiful, shiny black hair hanging down to his waist. He had come to Redskin Park to visit with special teams coach Wayne Sevier who dedicated a lot of his free time to working with the Native American community. Amused by my star-struck reaction, Wayne invited me to go to dinner with them and, of course, I accepted!

CHAPTER 69

Condom Sense and Sensibility

Whenever there was good stuff, the bad stuff was soon to follow. Mr. Hyde made another appearance today. Mr. Cooke had stayed in DC and everything started out nice and calm. He and Mrs. Cooke had gone to Duke's for lunch and returned to Marbella around 2. That's when things started to go south.

He called me at 2:45 and asked if a certain memo had gone out. I had typed it up the day before, after he had left for the day, and since I knew he wasn't coming back to the Park today, I put the memo, along with other important stuff, on today's shuttle run to DC so he could sign and return it to me for distribution. To me, this made perfect sense, because I knew he wasn't coming out to the Park tomorrow either. Of course, what made sense to me hardly ever made sense to Mr. Cooke.

When I told him what I had done, the proverbial crap hit the fan. He said I should have held onto the memo so I could sign and send it out for him, loudly adding to the same sentence "NEVER DO THAT AGAIN" and "AREN'T YOU SOMETHING" (the hair on the back of my neck was standing straight up). What I wanted to tell him was "Chill JKC, there's no need to get your Depends all in a twist", but instead, I calmly explained to him that the memo was in my computer and all I had to do was print another copy, to which he impatiently and angrily replied "WELL, YOU DO IT IMMEDIATELY".

Ayayay! Was I going crazy? Why did he get so upset over such minor details? One minute I would be humming along 70 mph thinking I was doing a great job, going the extra mile, and suddenly Mr. Cooke would throw a block that a linebacker would be proud of and blast you for no good reason. If I deserved it that would be one thing, but dammit, I didn't!

The only thing I could count on was that any time Mrs. Cooke got Mr. Cooke all pissed off, he would find a way to take it out on me. I wondered, was there an ASPCA for secretaries? Wasn't there someone I could call?!?

I still had a little over an hour before I could quit for the day and I felt like a sitting duck waiting for the next barrage of gunfire. I could hear him going off at one of his secretaries at Kent Farms about Mrs. Cooke's credit card bills. Reviewing every single charge listed on Mrs. Cooke's credit card statements was one of the secretary's responsibilities. After she finished her review, she would then forward the statements on to Mr. Cooke for his approval to pay. There was one particular statement this month that showed excessive charges at the Chanel Boutique and, the real reason Mr. Cooke was going nuts, mysterious charges from a couple of pricey hotels in West Virginia and, finally – and this one took the cake — a charge from a store called "Condom Sense". Now, how "in your face" was that? I just knew deep down that Mrs. Cooke had deliberately put the charges on her card just to get Mr. Cooke's goat. "Hmm", I wondered to myself, "what do the Kent Farms staff list condoms under, miscellaneous maybe?"

CHAPTER 70

Answer the phone properly! or To Pee or Not To Pee?

I spent Thanksgiving with my sister, Patty, and her husband, Butch, in Vermont. I had spent several years in Vermont and loved it for its peace and beauty and, of course, the excellent skiing. We had a great visit and, like everyone else, drank and ate way too much. The weekend was over in a flash. Patty dropped me off at the Lebanon, NH airport and, as my plane lifted up into the clouds, I watched Vermont disappear beneath me.

A couple of hours later, we touched down at National and, while I was waiting by the baggage claim, I spotted journalist Sam Donaldson, who was sitting all by himself, apparently waiting to meet up with someone. I knew he had been trying without success to get an interview with Mr. Cooke for the TV news magazine "*Prime Time*". He didn't seem to be too busy with anything, so I went up to him and introduced myself and said I was sorry Mr. Cooke had turned down his requests for an interview. He was very nice and said he was going to try again. He also mentioned the fast approaching Super Bowl and the Redskins' shaky chances of getting there this time. I agreed that we would have to work a little harder to get there this year.

When I got home, I found a message from Mr. Cooke on my answering machine. He wanted me to call him back. I called him right away just to get it over with so I could relax for the rest of the evening. He must not have been able to talk, or whatever question he did have had already been answered, because the conversation went like this: Cat: "Hello Mr.

Cooke, it's Miss Crozier, I've just returned from Vermont." Mr. Cooke: "Yes, well, I'll see you tomorrow." Cat: "I'm returning your call, Mr. Cooke, was there something you needed?" Mr. Cooke: "No, it's been taken care of. Bye bye". Not even "welcome back" or "thanks for returning my call". But that was fine with me; he didn't need anything and now I could relax.

Today, while I was in the bathroom, Mrs. Cooke called. She was going out and wanted to know where the new driver/houseman was so she could call him back to Marbella in case Mr. Cooke, who was at home and in bed with a cold, needed him while she was out. Apparently, she didn't like the way my phone was answered (I found this very amusing) and ended up complaining to Mr. Cooke who then raked me over the coals for ASSUMING my desk-sitter knew how to answer a telephone. He demanded to know "who was at my desk when I was PRESUMEDLY in the ladies' room". I thought, oh my God, what does this man want from me??? This was so ridiculous. Smiling to myself, I informed him the person who answered the phone was BJ, the receptionist who had been in charge of the switchboard for Redskin Park for the past several years! Silly me, ASSUMING that she knew how to answer phones. But Mr. Cooke continued, and told me that ASSUMING things was one of my biggest faults and because of that, I had got him into trouble many times. So, after that, I had to give an "Answering Phones 101" class to anyone who was kind and brave enough to cover my desk.

On the morning of December 3, I had a little fun with Desmond Howard (this year's Heisman Trophy winner and rookie Redskin). I walked into the kitchen to get some coffee and there were several of the players, Desmond among them, chowing down on whatever food was there. He had on gray sweat pants but they were only pulled up halfway and the pants he had on underneath were doing a poor job of covering his butt. So I said "hey Desmond, pull your pants up. We all know you have a nice hiney but we don't want to see it this early in the day!". Everyone cracked up.

After I got back to my desk and settled in for the day, Mr. Cooke called and asked me to come to Marbella because he still had a cold and wanted to work. Bummer! When I arrived, he asked me to come into his bedroom, where he was all cozy in his bed with a warm, cheerful fire in the fireplace. We worked for about an hour and I left to return to Redskin Park to finish some letters that I would send to him later in the day via the shuttle. The minute I stepped into my office at the Park, he called me and said he thought it would be good if I – not the shuttle - delivered the letters back to him; and besides, he wanted to dictate another "important" letter.

Crap! I didn't want to make another trip to Marbella! Not having any choice, I got everything done, locked up my office and drove to Marbella for the second time that day. My visit lasted no more than an hour. The "important" letter Mr. Cooke wanted to dictate turned out to be a draft of a short letter which he decided he didn't need until after the weekend.

While I was at Marbella, Mr. Cooke asked me to get some things out of his storage closet for him (potential Christmas gifts for various employees and family members). He kept a huge gift list as he always liked to give everyone gifts at Christmastime. Mrs. Cooke would be of no help. He sat at his desk, looked at the list, and, as he held it against his forehead with his crippled, arthrytic hand, said "She (Mrs. Cooke) ought to be helping me with this". I was relieved when he set the list aside and said he'd wait for Mrs. Cooke to return from her afternoon shopping.

CHAPTER 71

How to impress your friends

Today was game day and it was cold and blustery. I gathered up a pot of my homemade minestrone and headed over to Hal's for a nice quiet Sunday afternoon supper and to watch the Redskins play the Giants. After the game was over (we had won), I was getting ready to leave when Hal's phone rang. Hal's son, Peter, answered the phone and I was very surprised when he said the call was for me. I wondered who in the world would be calling me there, let alone even know I was there? As Peter handed me the phone, he said he thought it was Mr. Cooke. And it was.

There were actually two people who knew where I was that afternoon: my parents. And they only knew because I had spoken with them right before I left for Hal's. I shouldn't have been that surprised because whatever Mr. Cooke wanted, he got. He had got no answer at my place, so he called my parents and they told him I was at Hal's and then, somehow, he got his hands on Hal's phone number. Now that was spooky! The reason he wanted to get hold of me was that he had decided to make a press announcement about new plans for the stadium to be built in DC and he needed me to come to Marbella the next afternoon.

If you ever want to impress friends, watch an NFL game at their house and then have the team owner call you there from the stadium.

CHAPTER 72

The art of the deal

As requested by Mr. Cooke the day before, I arrived at Marbella in the afternoon to work on the DC stadium announcement. At first it was just Mr. Cooke, his general counsel and other corporate staff. Then we were joined by several prominent DC officials. Mr. Cooke got right down to business and was about as subtle as a Tyrannosaurus Rex that hadn't eaten in two weeks. In no uncertain terms, he told the DC guys he wanted to get a press release out THAT NIGHT and he needed them to GET THE MAYOR'S APROVAL RIGHT NOW! Mr. Cooke had really put them on the spot and they obviously weren't accustomed to being ordered around like that. They tried to get him to give them at least 24 hours, because the Mayor was "out of town and they weren't sure they could reach her".

Jack Kent Cooke, master of the deal, would have none of it and told them if they really needed to get hold of the Mayor they would know how to do it. He had laid his cards on the table. Everything got quiet and, after the DC officials' eyes met in silent exchange, one suggested to another that he try to reach the Mayor right then and there. Sure enough, his call found its target and the Mayor approved the announcement. The press release was issued that evening and I stayed at Marbella to help prepare additional paperwork.

That was the first time I had actually seen Mr. Cooke nail a deal, and I had to admit, I was impressed. When Mr. Cooke wanted something, he was a formidable force to be reckoned with.

The DC folks appeared to be happy with the deal. After all, they wanted the Redskins to play in Washington — not Maryland or Virginia. There was one sensitive subject that remained, however: the fate of the old RFK Stadium which had been the Redskins' home for the past 30+ years. They planned to raze RFK, but they didn't want to come right out and say that because a lot of people would object for sentimental reasons.

I worked at Marbella until 8:30 that night and hadn't been offered anything to eat or drink. Though a formal coffee service had been set up in the library for Mr. Cooke and his guests, I dared not touch it without a personal invitation from Mr. Cooke.

The day after the DC deal was announced, Mr. Cooke once again ruled the media and savored every minute of it. He showed up at Redskin Park about 11 am and held court in his office, giving one interview after another with TV, radio and newspaper reporters. The procession of reporters went right through my office and I had fun chatting with the same reporters I saw on TV every night. Mr. Cooke put on a real show for everyone. He ruled his kingdom and barked at his lowly serfs every chance he got. He was short with me and made up things to get after me about so he could show off. I could tell the reporters sympathized with me – they all knew his M.O.

CHAPTER 73

BUZZ BUZZ BUZZ!!!

In spite of the bad weather — 4 inches of snow and ice on the roads – Mr. Cooke still came out to Redskin Park. He was very hyper and I wondered how much coffee he had consumed that morning. It was one of those days where he had me jumping through one hoop after another. Buzz... buzz... buzz went the intercom!!! Before I could make it back to my desk after the first buzz, he'd put his finger on the blasted buzzer again! I really thought he was doing it on purpose just to see how silly he could make me look. It was so ridiculous even I was laughing.

At one point Mr. Cooke told me to call Mrs. Cooke and tell her something. As soon as I got her on the phone he impatiently buzzed me over and over again. As fast as I could, I finished my call with Mrs. Cooke (not an easy thing to do since she spoke slowly and was hard to understand) and ran back into Mr. Cooke's office. He looked at me with this amazed look on his face and exclaimed, as if I had been missing for a couple of hours, "where have you been?" When I told him I had been on the phone with Mrs. Cooke, as he had requested, he said "well you shouldn't take so long". Yowza! I wanted to strangle him!

In the middle of all the chaos, Mr. Cooke entertained himself by participating in a Sotheby's jewelry sale, something he did quite often. He liked to buy expensive baubles for Mrs. Cooke (I was convinced they were more like rewards he kept on hand for Mrs. Cooke, to get her to come back home after she ran away). Mr. Cooke was so jovial that he even spent several minutes speaking with a woman who had dialed his direct number by mistake <u>three</u> times in a row. Lucky for her he was in such a good mood!

Mr. Cooke left around 3 o'clock, and on his way out the door, seeing it was still snowing, he looked at me and said "you should go home early, dear". Yeah right, fat chance — I glanced at my desk. It looked like an F5 tornado had blown through my office. I told him I had too much work to do but thanks anyway. The next day the weather was still bad. Mr. Cooke stayed home, I got caught up on my work and Redskin Park closed at 3:00. (This was the big nor'easter of '92 which wreaked havoc all up and down the east coast.)

CHAPTER 74

"Now it's my turn"

Before he arrived at Redskin Park, Mr. Cooke had already made up his mind that I wasn't going to do anything right today. He had his game plan, he had made up his rules du jour, and he had already won. Game, set and match. He showed up around 10:00 and went right to work. I spent a couple of hours at his desk, taking dictation, sorting through fan mail, etc. Mr. Cooke's goal was to clear the mess off of his desk and move it all to my desk. The phone rang non-stop and the faxes poured in.

A phone message for Mr. Cooke had been faxed from Kent Farms. I didn't take the message in right away because I knew he was on a private call and wouldn't appreciate the interruption. By the time he was off his call and got the message, it was about an hour old. Right away, he buzzed me and launched into a rage, ranting and raving at me and ending with his usual "I COULD KILL YOU".

After I took the message into Mr. Cooke's office, Coach Gibbs rounded the corner and came into my office to see Mr. Cooke. Mr. Cooke was still chewing me out over the phone and Joe could hear him. He gave me a sympathetic look and discreetly backed out into the hallway to hang out until the coast was clear. He had sympathy for me written all over his face. When it was all over, he came back into my office, leaned down towards me and said quietly "now it's my turn" and disappeared into Mr. Cooke's office. When he came out he came right over to me and whispered "well, I got mine too". I told him "No! No way, not after your incredible win over the

Cowboys!" He answered "We're both in the same boat as far as Mr. Cooke is concerned."

A couple of days later, when we passed in the hallway, Coach Gibbs pointed his finger at me and then quickly turned it into a thumbs-up. After that day, whenever we saw each other, we shared camaraderie and acknowledged each other with a knowing smile or nod of the head. I felt really lucky to have Joe Gibbs as a friend.

Mr. Cooke's mood was no better the next day and he picked on me all day long. In the morning he chewed me out twice because I couldn't read his mind(!). By the afternoon, my insides were churning, I had no patience left, and he was pushing me closer and closer to the edge. Pretending I was Dorothy, I tried clicking my heels together three times and told myself "I really like working here at Redskin Park . . . I really like working here at Redskin Park . . .". If I could just find a way to put up with Mr. Cooke everything would be okay!

CHAPTER 75

et tu Brutus?

Yesterday, I had to forward my Christmas bonus check (yay! I was finally getting one!) and letter on to Mr. Cooke at Marbella so he could sign them and then personally present them to me. Recently, I had had what I thought was a *private* conversation with one of the Kent Farms secretaries, who had told me she was pretty sure my bonus would be $1,000. So, when I saw that the check was made out for $250, I was confused. Thinking I knew her well enough and could trust her, I called her and asked if the bonus amounts had been lowered, because mine was small compared to what she had told me earlier. HUGE MISTAKE!

This morning, the Kent Farms office manager, the same woman who had interviewed me, called and was very upset with me. What I thought had been a very private conversation with my "friend" had been reported to her. Of course, she had misinterpreted the whole thing and made me feel like I was greedy and unappreciative and said I was tossing Mr. Cooke's personal gift to me back into his face because it wasn't enough. Actually, considering all the crap I had put up with for the last year, no amount was enough. Everything got blown way out of proportion. I wasn't a greedy person; on the contrary, I was incredibly generous. After about 10 minutes, the manager ended our one-sided discussion by saying Mr. Cooke knew everything and he was "enormously upset" with me.

My insides went cold. I was mortified. I didn't know whether to throw up or die. How in the world could this have happened? What in the world had possessed my so-called "friend" to tell the manager about our "private" conversation? I didn't know what to do. I was a total wreck and expected to be fired on the spot. I wanted desperately to avoid a face to face confrontation so I typed a note to Mr. Cooke in which I apologized over and over again. I faxed it to Marbella and also put a copy on his desk at Redskin Park so it would be the first thing he saw when he arrived.

Luck was with me and, as happened many times with Mr. Cooke, the obvious and expected never happened. He showed up in a great mood, went to his desk, read my note and told me it wasn't necessary and he understood completely. And it was over. Just like that.

Except for a quick trip home to New Jersey, for Christmas with my parents, the next couple of weeks passed by quietly. Ironically, as of January 6, I still had not received my bonus. Mr. Cooke had given me the letter but the check was missing. I guessed he kept forgetting to look for it at Marbella. He eventually gave it to me.

CHAPTER 76

Right answer, wrong person

Mr. Cooke was writing a letter to one of the executives of the NFL to express his opinion about who the NFL should hire as their TV contract negotiator. In the letter, he wanted to mention the name of one of Eddie Murphy's movies, but he couldn't think of the title. He called Mr. John into his office and asked him about it and Mr. John said "oh, the one about the king in New York". Right away I knew which movie they were talking about and I called out from my office "Coming to America"! Well! You would have thought I had farted loudly or something. Everything got quiet and Mr. Cooke gave me the most imperious look and said "YOU NEVER MIND; YOU JUST DO YOUR WORK". He then looked at Mr. John to find out the name of the movie. He just couldn't accept that the monkey – and not the organ grinder – knew the answer. (One of his favorite sayings, which he lived by, was by Winston Churchill: "NEVER TALK TO THE MONKEY WHEN THE ORGAN GRINDER IS IN THE ROOM".)

Ten minutes later Mr. John popped his head into his father's office and cheerfully said "I've got it Dad, it's 'Coming to America'". Mr. Cooke was delighted that Mr. John had found the answer. Now that he had got the information from the right person, he could finish his letter.

CHAPTER 77

Kill the messenger!

The first week of February had been tougher than usual. Mr. Cooke had been in a rotten humor because Mrs. Cooke was driving him crazy again. A couple of weeks ago, she and her sons left Marbella and moved back to Alexandria.

On Monday afternoon, after Mr. Cooke had left for home, Mrs. Cooke called for him at Redskin Park. Right away I thought to myself "oh crap, here we go again" and told her he had left and was in his car. She mumbled a little bit and said something to the effect that she had tried calling him in his car but the call wouldn't go through. This was her way of saying she was making a half-hearted attempt to call him and that she really didn't want to talk to him. Knowing Mr. Cooke always went bananas when she called, I begged her to hold on while I called him to tell him she was calling. Once she was on hold, I called Mr. Cooke and, when I relayed Mrs. Cooke's obviously bogus remark that she was "having trouble calling him in his car", he barked at me "Well? Is she calling the right number?". Yikes! A loaded question! Who was I to assume she knew her husband's car phone number? Especially when she was never far from a complete, super dooper, updated daily, special deluxe edition of the Cooke home/car phone directory. So, I told him yes, I had confirmed she was dialing the correct number. But he was still nasty and barked orders at me to have her call him IMMEDIATELY. Yes sir! Right away sir!

Thankful she was still on the line, I s-l-o-w-l-y repeated the number to her and asked her to please call him because he was now expecting her call. I hung up and, as hard as I could, willed her to call him, but deep down I knew she wouldn't because she had insisted on giving me a message that she was canceling their dinner plans for the evening. She wanted me to do her dirty work. He was going to kill me, the unfortunate messenger of the hurtful message, for sure! I fortified myself with a mug of hot chocolate and, after 15 minutes, I took a deep breath and called Mr. Cooke and gave him the message. I braced myself for the explosion and the death threats but, miraculously, none came. He whispered "ok" and hung up.

Yesterday brought no change in Mr. Cooke's demeanor. He was nasty and rude, and again, Mrs. Cooke was at the center of it. He was clearly in misery, and at one point, while I was sitting across from him at his desk, he put his elbows on the desk and dropped his head into his hands and said to me "you know she's driving me crazy, you know that". He was completely befuddled. He just couldn't think, he was so distracted. He kept shuffling papers around on his desk but didn't do anything with them. I would have felt sorry for him if he hadn't been so awful to me.

Unable to get any work done, Mr. Cooke focused all his attention on me. He would tell me to do something and then follow me around and watch me work, questioning everything I did and then objecting, saying I wasn't doing what he told me to do. Over and over again he did this until I thought I would lose my mind!

Eventually, like all other living creatures on this good earth, I had to go to the bathroom and I knew that would get him even more upset. I called him on his intercom and, making an effort to make my voice sound as natural as possible, told him I'd be away from my desk for a moment. He distractedly answered "why don't you get an intern to take care of whatever it is". I responded "I'd like to go to the ladies room Mr. Cooke", and he yelled "WELL HURRY UP!". Ah, what a pleasant person. If only I didn't need to work for a living!

Today, Mr. Cooke seemed to be in a better mood but he still required delicate handling. Unfortunately, his new driver/houseman had suddenly quit. He had called me earlier and told me he didn't want to work for Mr. Cooke anymore. . . he didn't want Mr. Cooke to try to call him . . . and he never wanted to hear Mr. Cooke's voice again. I laughed to myself and understood completely.

Mr. Cooke was in his car and I called him and told him about the houseman and he returned to Marbella to check on the situation. After a while, he called and kept me on the phone for what seemed like forever while he speculated on what could have happened with the houseman. He made observations and posed questions — all rhetorical, the last of which was a question. There was a long, uncomfortable silence and because we were on the phone, I thought well, maybe he's waiting for me to answer his question. Someone had to say something! So, not being able to help myself, I said "I don't know".

It was just what Mr. Cooke was waiting for. He jumped right on it and yelled "OF COURSE YOU DON'T KNOW, IT WAS A RHETORICAL QUESTION. YOU KNOW WHAT RHETORICAL MEANS DON'T YOU?" Insulted, I said "I was just conversing with you Mr. Cooke" (another big mistake!). He said "CONVERSING? I DON'T WANT CONVERSATION!" I was digging a hole so fast for myself I was gonna end up in China before I knew it. There was nothing I could do but laugh and think "Well then, so why are you keeping me on the phone if you don't want conversation?" But that wasn't possible, so I stayed quiet and he started all over again, talking about the houseman. I let him have his "conversation" with himself.

CHAPTER 78

No response, no raise

There were some really nice townhouses and condos going up near Redskin Park and I wanted to buy one of them. I was tired of living in an apartment and paying someone else's mortgage. It was time to buy. There was just one small obstacle: in order to complete the initial paperwork, I needed to tell the bank my expected income for the coming year. Oh boy, I thought, this is gonna be good. I wrote Mr. Cooke the following letter:

> *"Dear Mr. Cooke,*
>
> *On Monday February 15, I have a meeting with my prospective mortgagor for a new home in Ashburn. As you can imagine, they want to know all my financial information. This would include any raises I might receive this year. I last received a raise on January 1, 1992 and would like to know if I can expect another one soon. Thank you for your consideration.*
>
> *Best,*
> *Miss Crozier"*

My letter had fallen on deaf ears. Mr. Cooke never responded. And I never got a raise. I must have been crazy to think he would actually have been supportive of my efforts to buy my first home.

CHAPTER 79

Phone-itis; good news, bad news

This morning at about 11 o'clock, Mr. Cooke's new houseman called from Marbella. I had to put him on hold while I took care of another call and before I could get back to him he hung up. I returned his call and Mr. Cooke answered the phone. He asked what I wanted and when I told him I was returning the houseman's call, he proceeded to lecture me non-stop for a solid ten minutes about how the houseman was "making too many phone calls . . . what did he want this time . . . how often did he call me . . . what did he want when he called me . . . he has PHONE-ITIS . . . didn't I realize that . . . why was I calling him back . . . I was being too nice . . . other staff have no problems giving orders to the houseman and they don't let the houseman take advantage of them . . . I let people take advantage of me and therefore Mr. Cooke".

Oh my god! Talk about PHONE-ITIS! Another long "yes sir"/"no sir" session, all for innocently returning the houseman's call.

Interestingly, during the one-sided phone conversation, Mr. Cooke mentioned that he was considering giving me a raise (yes! finally!) BUT that he was also considering whether or not he should keep me! (oh crap!) Kind of like "here's the good news" and then "here's the bad news". Now that I knew him as well as I did, I honestly didn't think he would fire me. He liked my work too much and I was pretty sure he liked me, in spite of what he said. Besides, who else at Redskin Park would he have to yell at? His bark was fierce but he didn't bite unless he had no choice. But what a cruel thing to say to me. Especially when I was trying to buy a house.

CHAPTER 80

Goodbye Joe, hello Richie

At about 7 o'clock Friday morning, while I was in my kitchen making coffee for my visiting parents and myself, I heard something on the radio about Coach Gibbs resigning. What??? I couldn't believe my ears! Mr. Cooke had sure kept that one under wraps. Knowing I'd be needed at the Park ASAP, I quickly showered and dressed and left. All of the radio stations were talking about it. The Park was swamped with media. This was huge.

Mr. Cooke soon arrived and we went right to work on his remarks for the press conference scheduled for 2:00 that afternoon. He had nothing but kind praise for Gibbs and also for Richie Petitbon, whom he had asked to step into Gibbs' huge sneakers. Mr. Cooke seemed to be taking it all in stride.

At exactly 1:59, I followed Mr. Cooke, Mr. John and and Coach Gibbs down the hall to the auditorium for the press conference. The hallway was all lit up by the press and all the cameras zoomed in on the three men's faces. Regular TV programming was pre-empted. One would have thought the President of the United States had resigned! The press conference lasted one hour and afterwards, in his office, Mr. Cooke gave one-on-one interviews with the reporters.

In hindsight, all of the meetings Mr. Cooke had been having recently with Joe Gibbs, Richie Petitbon and Mr. John now made make sense. Especially when I remembered Richie Petitbon standing in my office (evidently right after Mr. Cooke had offered him the job of his dreams) looking as if he'd been hit in the head with a 2x4.

All of us at the Park hated to see Joe go. We would miss him terribly. In the short time I had worked with him, I had grown to like and deeply respect him, not just as the Redskins coach, but as a human being.

A few days after Petitbon was named new head coach, Mr. Cooke asked me to get him on the phone. Richie wasn't in his office, so I asked his secretary to find him right away and have him return Mr. Cooke's call. Then I buzzed Mr. Cooke and told him "Coach Petitbon will call you shortly, I have someone looking for him". He said "okay" and hung up.

A couple of seconds later Mr. Cooke buzzed me back and launched into an outburst: "DO YOU KNOW WHAT YOU JUST SAID? WHEN YOU SAID 'COACH PETITBON WILL CALL YOU SHORTLY', WHAT YOU REALLY SAID WAS COACH PETITBON IS TOO BUSY TO TALK TO YOU RIGHT NOW BUT HE'LL CALL YOU SHORTLY. NOW NO COACH IN MY HISTORY OF TEAM OWNERSHIP HAS EVER BEEN TOO BUSY TO CALL ME. NOW YOU WATCH YOURSELF, YOUNG LADY, AND BE CAREFUL WHAT YOU SAY. PLEASE!"

Yes sir!

CHAPTER 81

Love is in the air

Mr. Cooke must have called me ten times over the weekend. He was all excited about going to New York City and Lexington KY this week. He was also excited about the front page article on him in Sunday's Washington Post. He was happy and that made me happy.

Saturday night, at about 7 pm, Mr. Cooke called me at home, from Marbella, and he was giddy as all get out. Mrs. Cooke had returned to Marbella to have dinner with him and it sounded like they were having too much of a good time. When I answered my phone, he sang out in a silly falsetto voice "hoo, hoo, hoo . . . whom do you think this is?" "Holy crap!" I thought, "What are the kids up to now?" He had nothing important to say to me, no real reason for his call, other than to share his happiness. I just couldn't figure this guy out. He truly was an enigma if ever there was one!

Mr. and Mrs. Cooke were going through another one of their reunion phases. She was accompanying him on his travels this week and he was like Antony, treating her like his Cleopatra. Nothing was too good for his wonderful wife! They stopped by the Park on their way to his plane and he was as silly as a 16 year old boy in love. To top it all off, he was so preoccupied, he had even left his wallet and hearing aide behind at Marbella. Luckily, the shuttle was making its stop at the Park so it was quickly dispatched to Marbella to pick up the forgotten wallet and hearing aide.

Oh man, I wondered, what were we all in for this time and how long would it last?

CHAPTER 82

A simple dialogue with JKC

One day, Mr. Cooke was really mellow, quietly working at his desk. I couldn't resist the rare opportunity to have a pleasant exchange with him. It went something like this:

Me:	That's a beautiful rose, Mr. Cooke
JKC:	Thank you
Me:	Have you smelled it sir?
JKC:	Yes. Is there anything else you would like me to do, dear?
Me:	Have you taken your medicine yet sir?
JKC:	No. I'll do that right now. Thank you, dear.

CHAPTER 83

Sorry Sir, she's left for the day

I wrote the following note to Mr. Cooke because I heard he had complained all weekend long to a Kent Farms secretary about his calling for me at 5:01 Friday afternoon, only to be told by the receptionist that I had just left. I was amused that he felt he needed to complain to the other secretary instead of just calling me.

> *"Mr. Cooke,*
>
> *I understand you called for me at 5:01 on Friday. I had to leave work on time that night because I had a 5:30 appointment. I'm sorry I missed your call. Most nights, I am in the office until at least 5:15 or so and many nights until at least 5:30. You should know, however, that when 5:00 o'clock comes, I do things such as wash your tea cup and tea carafe, do any necessary paper shredding, take care of outgoing mail, re-stock desk supplies, go to the ladies' room, etc — things that require me to be away from my desk.*
>
> *C"*

CHAPTER 84

Escape to Pemaquid

Maine was calling me. I desperately needed a break, the plane tickets were on sale, so why not? It would be a quick two-day visit and I would make every minute count. After the short, non-stop flight to Portland, I picked up my rental car and, within minutes, I was on my way to Pemaquid. After about 50 miles, I exited Route 1 North into the picturesque riverside town of Damariscotta. The town was draped in that grey, cold, wet veil that only a New England waterside town could have in the spring. I drove down the main street, passing some of my favorite shops. I could feel Renys Underground reaching out to me, but I didn't want to delay my arrival in Pemaquid by a single moment. Maybe I'd run into town the next day.

I turned onto Rt 130 and headed out towards the coast. 15 minutes later, I was on the Pemaquid Trail, a dead-end narrow road that skirted along the edge of John's Bay for about two miles. The Trail was the best kept secret in Maine — hardly anyone knew about it! Beautiful pine and white birch woods bordered the non-water side of the Trail. The water side was peppered with one charming salt box cottage after another, each with its own enchanting style and unique view of the bay. The water there was always alive; it changed every minute. Whether the tide was on its way in or out, gentle waves embraced the rocks and made soft whooshing noises – nature's perfect lullaby. I would take that over TV any day.

I pulled into my cousins' driveway. Their beautiful home was right on the water, its majestic views unmatched. I was very spoiled. Their door was always open to me and I visited as often as I could. Louise and her husband, Bob, met me at the door and greeted me warmly. Cocktail hour was under way and a welcoming fire was crackling in the big stone fireplace. Ahhh! It didn't get much better than that! With my first sip of scotch and Bob and Louise's excellent company, all of my cares and problems drifted out with the tide.

Of course, Louise and Bob wanted to hear all about what it was like to work for Jack Kent Cooke and I shared many of the peaks and valleys of my life with Mr. Cooke. After they got over the initial shock of what they had heard, they both asked me the same question everyone else asked me: "why don't you just quit?" I told them about the two year commitment I had made to myself.

That night, tucked away in the cozy loft with the window raised just enough so I could hear the water, I slept like a baby. It was the best sleep I had had in weeks. I awoke at dawn to the comforting, familiar sounds of the lobstermen and their boats making their early morning rounds and checking their traps for "keepers". The sunrise promised a beautiful spring day.

While most of the Trail's homeowners were still away doing their winter snowbird thing, a few had found their way back. The snow that had accumulated during the winter was steadily disappearing. Of the snowbirds who had returned early were Bob's sister, Betty, and her husband Dick, who lived next door. Early that afternoon, I decided to pay them a visit. As I walked past one of their kitchen windows, I noticed what appeared to be the handle of a pot or frying pan, newly revealed by the melting snow. I grabbed the handle and pulled it out of the snow. Sure enough, it was a medium sized pot which still contained the remnants of food that had been burnt beyond recognition. Puzzled, I wondered what that was that all about.

It was no secret that Betty was not very enthusiastic about cooking. She weighed no more than 90 lbs soaking wet and her idea of a big meal was a couple of leaves of lettuce topped with a couple of bites of lobster. Her oven went months and months between uses. We knew this, because the year before, her daughter had celebrated her 30th birthday there and Betty had put the leftover birthday cake in her oven just to get it off the counter and out of the way. And then everyone forgot about it. About four or five months later, her daughter came for another visit and, preparing to cook dinner, turned on the oven to pre-heat it. About 15 minutes later she started to smell a strange odor coming from the oven. She pulled down the oven door and looked inside and, to her utter amazement, saw a monstrous, undulating, blue and green pile of what turned out to be her several months old leftover birthday cake!

Abused and forgotten pot in hand, I knocked on Betty's door. Dick, a tall, thin, handsome silver haired, blue eyed man whose sun lined face told of many years spent on Maine's waters, answered the door. He spotted the pot in my hand and declared in his Maine accent "Yup, this is the time of the year I find 'em". He then explained, as if it were the most normal thing in the world, that whenever Betty burned a pot or pan during the winter, she simply tossed it out the window into the snow and forgot about it. I secretly wished I could be like that.

That afternoon, at 5 o'clock – cocktail hour – we visited with friends in their homes along the Trail and caught up on their news while taking in their own special and unique views of John's Bay. Then it was back to Louise & Bob's and their hearth and Louise's wonderful lobster stew – some good!

Before I knew it, it was time to leave. My escape had come to an end way too soon! How silly I had been to think it could last forever! It always broke my heart to turn my back to the water and leave that special place. However, I was always comforted by the fact that I knew I would return and, one day, build my retirement home there.

As I drove down 295 South towards the Portland Jetport, I could feel all the lightness and fun and relaxation drain out of me like blood flowing unchecked from a terrible wound.

Taking up the slack was the returning pressure of Mr. Cooke's unrelenting grip. I felt like an empty beer can being crushed in an offensive lineman's hand. How much pressure, I wondered, could I take before he squashed me like a bug? By the time my plane touched down in Jack Kent Cooke land, I had a ton of weight pressing down on me. All the pressure had returned. My jaw was clenched, my heart rate increased and my stomach filled with acid. The Christian had returned to the Coliseum.

CHAPTER 85

While the cat is away ...

I learned from the houseman that Mrs. Cooke's sons had been up to all sorts of mischief while Mr. & Mrs. Cooke were out of town this week. The two most serious offenses were taking out Mr. Cooke's brand new BMW and driving it all over the place, and helping themselves to the $400 that had been in the household cash box. I was so glad I wasn't there anymore! I had no desire to see what Mr. Cooke's reaction would be.

I had also heard that a couple of weekends ago Mrs. Cooke's younger son and a couple of his friends spent the weekend, unsupervised, at Kent Farms and damaged or destroyed just about everything they came in contact with. They ran over bushes and shrubbery with the golf cart; they messed around with Mr. Cooke's clothes and tracked in muddy footprints all over the luxurious white carpeting. I was horrified to hear they had even messed around with one of the farm's gas tanks. The cover had been left off and, unbelievably, burned matches had been scattered around the opening. When I heard about this, I remembered finding a lot of broken glass, an empty can of lighter fluid and several burned matches on the slate sidewalk around the side of the house towards Mr. Cooke's dressing room at Marbella. It was scary to think that a 13 year old boy was into this sort of insane activity. I couldn't say it enough: thank god I was out of there!

Mr. Cooke returned from his trip and came to work at Redskin Park. He was as pleasant as could be to everyone except me. From the moment he appeared in his office, he inundated me with all of his paperwork and everything else that had piled up during the past week, all the time complaining to me about things I should have done for him while he was away. Things like 1) I should have arranged to have his new BMW serviced at a dealership other than the one he had bought it from, because it would have been more convenient (I knew nothing about his cars, nor were they ever my responsibility); and 2) I didn't give him a summarization of the expenses covered by a reimbursement check (heck, I had never even seen the check, let alone the fact that all checks were issued by the Kent Farms staff).

Those complaints were nothing. I could have easily dealt with them. What really tortured me was that, after making each complaint, he said, in a teasing voice, "Mrs. X (the Kent Farms secretary) would have done that for me". But that wasn't all. For the rest of the day, whenever he asked me to do something, he followed it up loudly and clearly with "Now, if you can't do that, you let me know and I'll get Mrs. X to do it. That would sure embarrass you wouldn't it?"

In spite of all of Mr. Cooke's relentless badgering, I stayed late to get all of the loose ends cleaned up. He had driven me nuts today! I had seen him use that low and annoying tactic with other staff and it was demeaning, especially when you were already working your ass off. I hoped tomorrow would be a better day.

CHAPTER 86

Boss dearest

Mr. Cooke was worse than usual today, which means he was really, really awful! He showed up at the Park about 11:00 a.m. and looked terrible, like he'd been up all night. You could tell he was in a foul mood just by looking at him. When he set eyes on you, it put the fear of God in you. It wasn't surprising though. The storm clouds had been gathering for the past week and I knew it was just a matter of time before all hell broke loose. I knew Mr. Cooke was going to suck up whoever was in his path like a tornado and spit them out in pieces. I braced myself for the worst.

Within five minutes I got hell for:

1. not updating the phone directory from the green Jaguar and putting it in the new Jeep (explanation: the Kent Farms staff and I had been looking for that directory for the past two months, ever since Mr. Cooke gave the Jaguar to his son).

2. not telling him the phone number of the Jeep (explanation: the phone now in the Jeep came from the Taurus; he knew that).

3. he had to wait 30 seconds for me to appear in his office after he buzzed me (explanation: I was on the phone with Eugene McCarthy, at his request).

4. why hadn't I checked with him before letting the shuttle leave Kent Farms for Redskin Park? (explanation: if they valued their life, no one ever

disturbed him that early in the morning if they didn't know for sure that he was up).

5. I had taken a couple of faxes in to him while he was on the phone and I got a very grouchy look accompanied by a growl of "I didn't want you in here" (explanation: he had ordered me to bring him all messages immediately, as soon as they were received!).

At 2 pm, long after the shuttle had left the Park, Mr. Cooke buzzed me and said "now don't let the shuttle go without asking me this time". Crap! He knew the shuttle left at noon! So I said "Mr. Cooke, the shuttle left a long time ago". Then, in front of the executive staff who were in his office, he went off on me, saying things like "you're something else. . . look what you've gone and done now. . ." He never gave me a chance to remind him that, two hours earlier, when I did ask him if it was ok for the shuttle to leave, he had told me he "didn't give a damn".

His foul mood grew even worse and he called me back on the intercom three more times just to tell me I was "really something", hanging up on me each time before I could remind him that I had told him the shuttle was leaving! So, there I sat at my desk, mute, holding my head in my hands in total frustration. And on top of that, everyone who was in his office thought I was an idiot!

It was at this point I started counting the months and weeks and days until I could tell him to go to hell and just walk out of there and be free again. Six months to go . . .

CHAPTER 87

The Five O'Clock Club

About a week ago, I got initiated into the players' clandestine Five O'Clock Club. On the Friday of Mini Camp weekend, I went for a bike ride after work. I kept my bicycle in one of the maintenance sheds at the Park because the riding trail went right past there and I could ride directly from work. After my ride, I went to put my bike back in the shed and noticed the lights were on in the maintenance office, so I checked it out. I saw Jacoby, Bostic, Williams, Caldwell and Lachey, all sitting around drinking beer and just shooting the breeze. I didn't want to bother them, but when I turned to leave, they noticed me and waved me in. Before I knew it, I had a frosty long neck in my hand. I was hot and sweaty and thirsty from my ride and that beer looked awfully good.

We all agreed that what got said in the shed stayed in the shed. I knew that if Mr. Cooke ever found out I was in there it would have been the end of me for sure! According to the guys, the "club" was formed in the Riggins days and everyone thought it had been disbanded during the Gibbs era. We shared some laughs, I drank my beer and left.

CHAPTER 88

A new skill

Mr. Cooke continued to push my buttons. He had been so obnoxious during the first two weeks of May that it took every bit of my strength to keep from telling him to go screw himself. He was nasty and cranky and just itching for a fight. Nothing I said went without a hurtful, sarcastic reply from him. He paid no attention to anything I wrote or told him and then, when he needed the information, he'd get all pissed off because he was sure I hadn't given it to him.

Whenever he chewed me out he'd punctuate it by again resorting to that favorite tactic of his, saying that his Kent Farms secretary "wouldn't have done that" or "would have done that, she's so wonderful you know". More than anything, I wanted to tell him "if you think your Mrs. X is so wonderful, then get her to come work here!". This went on day after day after day. I didn't know if I could take it much longer.

Trying to get things done for Mr. Cooke was like trying to work with your hands tied behind your back. He expected you to get a lot done BUT you had to follow all of his little rules which were subject to change, without notification, on a daily basis.

On Friday, I had to go to Marbella where Mr. Cooke was having a big meeting. Once the cook had finished preparing and serving the food for the meeting, he just up and quit. He grabbed his bag and walked out. He couldn't take it anymore. As soon as Mr. Cooke's guests left, I told him the cook had quit. He must have expected it, because he took the news pretty calmly. I later learned that, apparently to save face, he told the Marbella staff he had *fired* the cook and told him never to come back again.

Because there was no longer a cook in the house, and because I was still there, I ended up helping the houseman wash and dry all of the dishes and crystal that had been used for the meeting. Another new skill for my resume.

CHAPTER 89

No SBXXVI ring for Cat

One week ago, DC Council Chairman John Wilson hanged himself and was found by his estranged wife, Bonnie. She had gone to his house to check up on him at the request of his office. There had been reports that he had suffered from depression. He hadn't even left a note. We were all speechless – even Mr. Cooke, for once – when we heard the tragic news. Wilson had been Mr. Cooke's go-to guy in the DC government and the two had worked closely together during the stadium negotiations.

Mr. Cooke's mood had improved from a couple of weeks ago and, oh man, was I grateful for that. A few days ago he found out that a former secretary of his, from his early Canada days, was sick and in the hospital. You would have thought it had been his mother! He couldn't do enough fast enough. He wanted all of her medical bills sent to him and he wanted her in a private room. Once she was released from the hospital he sent her a huge floral arrangement and letters via FedEx. And then he even sent her a SBXXVI ladies ring! This had struck a sour note with me because everyone in the Redskins organization – except me – had received a ring. That was a hard one for me to swallow.

CHAPTER 90

~~Murphy's~~ JKC's Law

As usual, Murphy's Law (it should really be called JKC's Law) struck at every opportunity. About 15 minutes before Mr. Cooke showed up this morning, I had shredded several drafts of a document, following his directions to shred each draft as soon as a new version had been done. Wouldn't you know it, the first thing Mr. Cooke asked me for when he picked up the new draft was the old one! Damn, a new rule! It was what it was. I looked at him and told him I had shredded the old drafts. He looked at me, puffed himself up and very dramatically exclaimed "NOW I WON'T BE ABLE TO GET THE DEAL DONE TODAY!".

I told him I could get a copy of the earlier draft from the west coast office in about 15 minutes (unless they had also shredded it!). But he wanted to be upset some more, so he continued with his rant, this time finishing with "I REALLY DON'T KNOW, MISS CROZIER, MAYBE YOU OUGHT TO BE LOOKING FOR ANOTHER JOB SOMEWHERE ELSE". I wanted more than anything to look him in the eye, lay all my cards on the table, call his bluff and say "fine, maybe I just ought to do that!". But I couldn't; I needed my job! I was terrified and didn't respond. I knew he was just blowing off steam and taking another cheap shot at me, but his insensitive comments had found their target and done their job.

Next, Mr. Cooke moved on to the subject of yesterday's shuttle run. He told me his mail had arrived late at Marbella and asked me why I just didn't hold everything at Redskin Park for him for today. I explained that, because he was planning to fly up to Belmont to watch one of his horses race today, I didn't think he'd be coming to the Park. I also told him I thought it would be best to send everything to Marbella to make sure he got everything he needed for Belmont. As usual, nothing I said was right. And he told me I was irresponsible for sending his mail to Marbella yesterday. Ayayay! Well, ok then, Mr. Cooke, if that was the case, why didn't you just bring it back to the Park with you? I guess that would have been too much trouble for you? I threw my hands up in the air and resigned myself to having one of those days where it was his game, his rules and his cheap victory.

CHAPTER 91

Dear Mr. Cooke...

I wrote Mr. Cooke the following note after he wrongly accused me of making changes to his servants' job descriptions or, as he called them, "duties". This was a good example of how such a small thing could take on huge proportions and cause all sorts of problems for several of Mr. Cooke's staff.

"Dear Mr. Cooke,
When you hired (X) to take (X's) place, I printed out the new Marbella Staff Duties, dated May 27.

I made no changes other than to substitute (X's) name with (X).

I then gave you the new printout for your review and approval to distribute. You gave me approval to distribute, which I did.

Shortly after you hired (X), (XX) told you he had the time to take on more duties. I distinctly remember you switching the duties in question to (XX) and then commending (XX) for his cooperation.

Unfortunately, I don't have any copies of the old duty lists that I can show you to offer proof of this.

Again, Mr. Cooke, I have made no unauthorized changes to the Marbella Staff Duties. I'm very sorry if you think otherwise.

As you requested, new staff duty lists will be made and distributed tomorrow to (X), (XX) and (XXX), at Marbella, via the shuttle. Mrs. (X) and Mrs. (XX) at Kent Farms will also receive copies.

C"

CHAPTER 92

The beginning of the end

After working for Mr. Cooke for 19 long months, I was beginning to have serious doubts as to whether I could go on working for him much longer. A continuous debate was raging inside my head. I was trying to buy a house; I needed stability; I needed to know that my future was secure. And did I really have a future here? Did I really want a future here? Over and over again I studied the pros and cons of staying or leaving. It was much easier to come up with "cons" than "pros" aside from the obvious privileges that came with being part of the Redskins organization.

Everything was approaching critical mass and something was going to have to give soon. Mr. Cooke and I had definitely come a long way together. I had stuck it out; I had grown a thicker skin and I had learned to turn a deaf ear to all of his endless, harsh and unfounded rantings. I was no longer afraid of him. I knew he had picked up on that and, feeling the need to keep me guessing, he was always looking for new ways to get to me. I was sure that his new strategy of constant, annoying nit picking was all about that. After a lot of soul searching, I tried to fix things one more time and wrote the following letter to Mr. Cooke.

> *"Dear Mr. Cooke,*
> *I don't give you 100% — I give you 200%.*
> *I'm on your side — no one else's.*
> *I do nothing that you do not tell me to do.*
> *I give you all I can possibly give, and somehow, find more to give when you ask.*

I have always taken pride in my work and who I work for. I've heard it said that people who are tops in their field all show confidence, but temper it with a small amount of humility. I have always been confident in my work and have shown maybe even a little too much humility.

But lately, my confidence has been greatly shaken by your words, angry words such as last night ("give you hell . . . utmost catastrophic stupidity I've ever had in my life"). You made me feel awful last night, when I had done nothing except follow your instructions. And I was very sorry that you had to return home to turmoil after a long day's hard work, when you should have been able to sit down, relax and enjoy a nice dinner with Mrs. Cooke.

I have feelings too, Mr. Cooke. And they get hurt very easily. I take great pride in pleasing people, especially you, as my boss.

As you would say, I am at sea. I could understand your anger if I didn't follow your instructions. But I cannot understand being lambasted for doing my job.

As you know, I have signed an agreement for construction of a new home (my first) in Ashburn, close to Redskin Park. I have incurred several non-refundable expenses. Before I invest any further in my new home, I ask you to decide if you really want me as your secretary. If you plan to fire me, please do so now before I close on my new home in September.

I'm not asking you for special treatment; I'm just asking that you treat me as a human being and respect me for the good employee that I am. In other words, please treat me fairly.

I love working for you and the Redskins. I thrive in a challenging environment, and working for you has not been a small challenge. But, if I can't keep you happy and feel good about my job, there's no sense in continuing such a relationship.

I only ask that, once again, you consider that I am not an independently wealthy person and I am very dependent on my job. If you decide to fire me, I would ask that I be kept on at Redskin Park in some capacity through the end of August, at which time the lease on my apartment will expire and I will relocate.

Sincerely,
Catherine Crozier"

I signed the letter and faxed it to Mr. Cooke at Marbella. A few minutes later, Mr. Cooke called me and said "You know, you never cease to amaze me. Why would you send this letter of yours by fax, where the whole staff here can read it? You stupid ass. I'll see you soon."

Later that day, still at Marbella, he called me back and continued the discussion, saying "I can't help that, that's the way I am. I'm 80 years old and I'm not going to change. You're going to have to change if you want to stay here. You talk too much. And I'm not the only one who has noticed that. Several people have told me. I only want you to say 'yes sir' and 'no sir'. I want no editorial from you. I had to tell my servants to stop calling you because you talk too much and take too long to say what you've got to say. You should get right to the point and then hang up. Can you do that? At least six or seven people have told me you slam things around and say things like 'he's impossible'. Are you going to stop that?" Wondering to myself if he had secret cameras installed in my office, I silently answered HELL NO!

Once again Mr. Cooke had resorted to his favorite tactic of turning staff against each other and making them paranoid. He told me we would talk tomorrow "about you and me" when he came out to Redskin Park.

The next day Mr. Cooke decided he had better put me on the defensive for our pending discussion about my letter. He accomplished this by buzzing me and asking me: "Have you had any problems with delayed delivery by the post office lately?" Unaware that the question was his opening move in his chosen game that day, I truthfully answered "No sir, I haven't". Wrong move! He had set the trap and I fell right in. When would I ever learn? The right answer, the one he wanted, was "yes sir". But how was I supposed to know that? Unwittingly, I had given him my honest answer which was no, I hadn't had any problems recently with the post office. Why in the world would I lie about something like that?

He looked at me, from his desk, for about 5 seconds and said, very seriously, that I "had better come into his office". The second I got in there he jumped all over me and accused me of contradicting him and that, whenever he asked me questions I should ALWAYS answer "YES SIR" or "NO SIR" and NEVER CONTRADICT HIM. And on and on he went. And to make matters even worse, his biggest yes man of all, his general counsel, sat there and, with a smug smirk on his face, told me that just the other day he had received a letter which took TEN days to get from DC to Middleburg. Yeah? Well, so what, you big brown-noser! What did that have to do with me?! I had answered Mr. Cooke's question truthfully. Again, Mr. Cooke repeated he wanted NO CONTRADICTIONS and that I should only answer "YES SIR" or "NO SIR" and to NEVER OFFER MY COMMENTARY. I thought "OK then, I'll repeat my answer: NO SIR!"

Mr. Cooke's cruel and outrageous tactic set the desired tone and gave him the perfect segue for our "talk". I ended up sitting in the chair opposite him, across that big sea of a desk, for the umpteenth time, uttering "yes sir" and "no sir" as he went on non-stop for what seemed like hours. If he had told me the moon was purple I would have told him "yes sir". If that's what he wanted, that's what he would get.

The master of intimidation continued his attack, reinforcing his effort to make me paranoid towards my co-workers. He told me how everyone was complaining about me (truth: everyone liked me!), that I talked too much (truth: when did I have the time to talk?), that I complained about him, that I was always slamming things around in my office, cursing at him under my breath (truth: he was partially right about that, I wasn't a robot for god's sake, and who would blame me?)

Our "talk" finally ended with him telling me he was not going to change and that I would be the one who would have to do the changing. And if I could change, I could stay. I did not respond.

When he was done, I dragged what was left of myself back to my desk. I left his office feeling worse than ever. I was totally defeated. Nothing had been resolved. He had every intention of continuing to be an irascible, obnoxious SOB and I could leave if I didn't like it!

I went home that night, terribly upset. I knew I had only promised myself I would stay with Cooke for two years, but somehow the idealist in me had hoped I could find the key to bring out the "good" Mr. Cooke and keep the "bad" Mr. Cooke away. I now knew that could never happen. I would have to cancel plans for my new home. I saw a lot of changes coming.

CHAPTER 93

Have a peanut

Mr. Cooke had stayed home for the day. Before I released the shuttle for its run to Marbella, I called him to find out if there was anything he wanted. I specifically mentioned a "gray envelope addressed to him from Kent Farms which looked like it had a check in it". He told me to hold that envelope at Redskin Park until the next day.

At about 12:30, Mr. Cooke called me from Duke's, where he was having lunch, and asked me if I had reserved his table for him. I told him no, because I didn't know he was going out to lunch. Without saying another word, he hung up. I waited about 15 minutes and called Duke's to find out what was going on and was told by the manager that Mr. Cooke had shown up unannounced and his table had already been taken, but luckily the table next to it was free. Then he told me if I needed any references for a new job to call him. I thought "What? What was he talking about?". Apparently, Mr. Cooke, the bully, had put on a show at Duke's about "my no good secretary who didn't reserve my table and I'm going to fire her".

I was busy working, enjoying the peace and quiet, when Mr. Cooke called at 4:20. He was upset that he didn't have the gray envelope (that I had told him about earlier and which he told me to keep at Redskin Park!). He launched into an all-out attack. I tried several times to remind him what he had told me to do with the envelope, but every time I tried, he cut me off and said I had told him it was an "envelope of paychecks". He continued his attack, saying "you didn't say it was marked 'personal and confidential' . . . how did you know there were paychecks in the envelope. . . you had assumed there were paychecks in the envelope. . . why do you do these things to me . . . you did not say it was marked personal and confidential. . . are you once again thumping things around on your desk because if you are you can leave this instant . . . all you had to say was 'it's a gray envelope marked personal and confidential' ".

And then, turning the intensity up another notch, he shouted "YOU JUST SHUT YOUR MOUTH AND GET YOUR STUPID ASS DOWN HERE WITH THAT ENVELOPE". Then another order: "YOU BETTER GET IN YOUR GODDAMN CAR AND BRING IT DOWN HERE. I'M GOING TO TALK TO YOU TOMORROW. THIS HAS GONE TOO FAR, MRS. CROZIER." Then "DON'T YOU BE SLAMMING THINGS AROUND ON YOUR DESK. . ." Then "YOU GET YOUR ASS OFF THAT CHAIR AND COME DOWN HERE RIGHT NOW".

No one had ever spoken to me like that! No one, not ever! I numbly gathered up the freaking gray envelope and drove the 35 miles (in rush hour traffic) to Marbella. When I arrived, I didn't know what to expect, but at that point, I didn't care anymore. Freedom was looking awfully good.

I found Mr. Cooke, sitting at his desk in his library with a glass of wine and a bowl of peanuts, talking on the phone. He was calm. I set the gray envelope on the desk in front of him. He motioned to me to sit down. After about five minutes he finished his call and, as if nothing had happened, looked at me and cheerfully said "have a peanut".

He thanked me for bringing the envelope (like I really had a choice) and remarked "the drive in was nice, wasn't it?" (yeah, just lovely, Mr. Cooke, and what planet are you from?). Then he leaned towards me and very quietly said "please don't do my thinking for me". I said "yes sir" and after about ten minutes he dismissed me, adding "have another peanut". I wanted to pick up that bowl of peanuts and throw it at him as hard as I could.

CHAPTER 94

I'm going to kill you

First thing this morning, Mr. Cooke called and told me that if Mrs. Cooke (who was again absent from Marbella) called after he left for his meeting, I was to tell her he was in meetings in downtown DC and get a number where she could be reached after he was done with his meetings. All the usual alarms went off in my head. The mention of Mrs Cooke's name meant trouble. No matter what happened, I would end up in hot water.

So, when Mrs. Cooke called before Mr. Cooke left for his meetings, I put her call through. Wrong!!!

15 minutes later, a very angry Mr. Cooke called and told me I hadn't listened to him and, as usual, I got his message all screwed up, that he didn't want to talk to Mrs. Cooke and that I was to simply tell her he was in meetings and to get a number. He told me that he had taped the instructions he had given me, if I wanted him to play it back, and that if he had to record tapes every time he gave me instructions, I could leave right then and there. He got louder and louder and continued: "YOU THINK YOU'RE A SUPREME INTELLECT. WELL, I'LL BE THE FIRST TO TELL YOU YOU AREN'T. OH, I COULD KILL YOU FOR THIS ONE. YOU RUIN MORE OF MY DAYS THAN ANYONE I'VE KNOWN IN MY LIFE. YOU JUST RUINED ANOTHER DAY FOR ME. I DID NOT WANT TO TALK TO HER — YOU KNOW THAT. YOU HEARD ME. AND AS USUAL YOU BOTCHED THE DAMN THING FOR ME. WHY? WHY? JESUS CHRIST ALMIGHTY. GODDAMN YOU, CROZIER, I'M GOING TO KILL YOU WHEN I GET

THERE. I WON'T DO THAT THOUGH. ARE YOU DOING IT ON PURPOSE? I GIVE UP. I'LL SEE YOU AT 2:30."

And that was only half of his evil spew. I was done. I had nothing left. I couldn't take it anymore. I decided to focus on making the necessary preparations so I could get the hell out of there.

CHAPTER 95

Back to Alta's: the pig roundup

As soon as Friday rolled around I put Dickens in the car and drove up to Alta & Dave's for the weekend. I was at my breaking point and I needed R&R and the company of my good friends. I was traumatized. I had been beaten down, my confidence and self esteem taken away from me. I didn't even know how to laugh or have fun anymore. When I got out of my car, they took one look at me and knew I was hurting. They fed me, they listened to me, and they did their best to try to cheer me up. Even sweet little Katie got into the act and curled up on my lap.

By Sunday I was feeling better. Alta and I hopped into her truck and we drove down to the local market to pick up some yummy things for breakfast. On our way back, Alta started to mention how weird it was that nothing strange or interesting had happened during my visit (crazy stuff happened every time I was there). She had barely finished saying the words when, out of nowhere, a runaway pig suddenly appeared on the road in front of us and then trotted off into an empty field. We couldn't believe it! We looked at each other and didn't have to say a word. We were in! We pulled off the road, jumped out of the truck and went into pig roundup mode. Laughing hysterically, we herded the wayward pig up the hill and back to its home.

Whoever said "laughter was the best medicine" sure had that right. I had made an instant recovery! I returned home later that day, ready to face Mr. Cooke again.

CHAPTER 96

It's good to be the king

This week was quiet. Mr. Cooke came to Redskin Park for a few hours on Monday and a few hours on Friday, and made no appearances in between — much to my delight. However, "out of sight, out of mind" never applied to Mr. Cooke.

He was probably the only person in the world who could be in a good mood and be hateful at the same time. He criticized everything I did. He didn't like the way I answered his questions — the syntax wasn't quite right. In fact, that disturbed him so much that he got out his favorite reference on use of the English language and spent five minutes looking for an example to show me that I had used the wrong word.

I had taken something to him while he was working on the patio outside his office but, because my hands were full, I hadn't brought along my steno book; he told me to NEVER come to his desk again without my book. And again, hung up on syntax, he told me I didn't know how to properly use a thesaurus (hmm, I thought, so how did I get through college and write all my papers?). He told me I let the wind blow all of his papers around on the patio (what did he think would happen when he took the papers out of his briefcase and spread them on the table, in the wind?). He kept it up until he finally left for home.

He was a smart man; he had to know he was being ridiculous. What purpose did it serve other than to just be a bully? What was his game? Was getting me to quit his idea of winning? Was that what he wanted? I tried to let the false accusations and sarcastic comments bounce off of me, but it still frustrated the heck out of me that I couldn't defend myself for fear of bringing on another viscious attack.

I went into survival mode. I now saw the light at the end of the tunnel and I would plan my departure on my own terms.

I only had one more week to go until my vacation in Maine.

A couple of days before my vacation, Mr. Cooke was so pleasant that I actually started to get optimistic about my job again. I'd never learn. Later on, when I called him at Marbella to ask him if it was ok for the shuttle to leave Redskin Park, one of his house staff answered the phone. Five seconds later, he picked up the phone and said "hello Miss Crozier", to which I replied "hello Mr. Cooke, is it ok for the shuttle to leave?". He barked "you could have asked her (the housekeeper) and saved me a trip to the phone – YES!" and slammed down the phone.

He must have been having more problems at home, because when he was pissed off at home, I was the one who paid. Mr. Cooke gave new meaning to "reaching out and touching someone"! Recently he and Mrs. Cooke had been undergoing some sort of reconciliation (again). It was probably only because she wanted or needed something from him. Anyway, when she picked a fight with him and waltzed off to her apartment, the blood (most likely mine) would flow.

CHAPTER 97

Back to Pemaquid

It was finally time to head up to Maine for one whole glorious week, far away from Mr. Cooke. My plane took off from Dulles and headed towards Portland, and I left all my cares behind.

I made the familiar drive from Portland to Pemaquid in my rental car, full of anticipation and excitement. I could never get there fast enough! And when I finally made the turn onto the Pemaquid Trail and got my first look at the beautiful sparkling blue water of John's Bay, its surface covered with millions of diamonds at play in the brilliant sunlight, I was thrilled beyond words. It was like coming home. It was the only place I had ever been that, while I was there, I never got restless to be somewhere else. It was where I belonged.

My cousin always said that whenever I showed up, all sorts of extraordinary things happened, like big storms, normally reclusive seals and loons appearing, etc. And, right from the start, this visit was no exception. As I drove along the Trail to Louise's house, I saw a boat towing something really big, but mostly submerged, towards the Pemaquid beach. I pulled into the driveway, ran into the house, exchanged quick hugs and hellos with Louise and Bob, and bee-lined it for the binoculars that always hung next to the sliding glass door. I focused in on the boat and discovered it was towing a dead whale. Louise & Bob, knowing me too well, gave me a resigned look and shrugged their shoulders and said "see ya later". I grabbed my sunglasses and headed out the door to walk down to the beach. They knew it would be hours before they saw me again.

The whale was a young humpback, about 30 feet long. It had been towed to the beach where scientists from Woods Hole would perform a necropsy to determine the cause of death. Though I would much rather have seen it alive, joyfully spy hopping and leaping out of the water with members of its pod, I took advantage of the rare opportunity to get close and inspect the unfortunate lifeless creature that lay before me.

Shortly after the scientists arrived, but before they made their first cut, I left the beach to return to my cousin's house. I was definitely interested, but not enough to see a ton of whale guts spill out onto the beach. It sure was a good thing I left. When I got about 1,000 feet away, I was overwhelmed by the foulest odor I had ever come in contact with. It was all I could do to keep from throwing up. Grabbing anything I could to cover my mouth and nose and doing my darnedest not to breathe, I hurried down the Trail hoping to outrun the overpowering stink. I couldn't imagine what it was like for the folks performing the necropsy. Thankfully, I found relief as the Trail turned away from the direction of the wind.

After I cleaned up and changed my clothes, Louise, Bob and I stepped out onto the spacious deck with our glasses of iced tea. We moved our chairs around to nice, sunny spots and plopped down in them. We brought each other up to date and gazed out over the bright blue water cloaked in the dancing sunlight, its gentle rhythmic waves washing over the kelp and seaweed covered rocks. Even though they had lived in this very special place for several years, every day was like the first day there for Bob. Each day, he would go out on the deck or stand on the lawn, with his hands on his hips, and look out across the bay to the ocean and exclaim "Is this great or what!?" We lazily sat there for hours, it seemed, savoring every moment of the peaceful summer afternoon.

Cued by the five chimes of the antique Swedish clock that lived on the mantle over the fireplace, out came the scotch, Irish whiskey, gin, olives, ice cubes and drink glasses. It was 5 o'clock on the Pemaquid Trail, time for cocktails! Now, cocktail hour on the Pemaquid Trail was like going to church. It was serious business. Everyone was expected to attend and participate. Every day, on the stroke of 5:00, Betty and Dick, with scotch filled sterling silver flasks in hand, and their dachshund "Twink" in tow, would walk the tiny trail from their house to Louise and Bob's. All of the news, gossip and adventures of the past 24 hours would be shared, cigarettes would be smoked one after the other, hors d'oeuvres would be passed, and the drinks would be poured, one after another. It was a decadent life!

Mother Nature provided a beautiful sunset and, as the sky went from blue to steel blue to dark, an amazing, huge full moon rose above us and reflected down on the calm satiny water. It was perfectly still, not even a hint of a breeze. Bob, who loved music, especially classic jazz and big band, played one of his Ray Anthony albums. We danced in the moonlight and the ice cubes tinkled along the sides of our drink glasses. We all joined in and sang a drunken version of Ray Anthony's "The Talk of the Town". It was a night to remember.

I was determined to finally swim in the freezing waters of John's Bay. I had already tried so many times it was ridiculous. Every time my feet touched that icy water I backed out faster than a fart empties an elevator. Today was the day. My mind was made up. It was hot and there wasn't a cloud in the sky. If I didn't get in today, I'd never get in. It was do or die. Go big or stay at home. Determined, I threw on my bathing suit, grabbed a towel and walked down to the beach. I sat on my towel and stared at the water. I figured that, if I sat there long enough, I'd get so hot I'd have to go in. The first part worked. The second part didn't work so well. It took a long, painful 20 minutes to get in up to my knees, and then everything from my knees down went completely numb. Who was I kidding? I was never gonna get in that water! I returned to my towel, defeated. Maybe next summer . . .

My week went by in a flash. It was time to return to Virginia and finish things up with Mr. Cooke.

CHAPTER 98

Welcome back!

Refreshed from my time in Maine, I cheerfully greeted Mr. Cooke when he arrived at Redskin Park and, instead of returning the greeting or saying "welcome back" or "did you have a nice time?", he started right in on me, saying he had had three separate complaints during the last week about me swearing over the phone. I thought, "okay, so we're gonna go right at it again, are we?".

What in the heck was going on? Was he taping my phone calls? I was human after all. I wasn't a saint and I didn't deny I could come up with some choice words when I needed to. But who didn't? .

Mr. Cooke continued his attack, yelling "YOU ARE NOT BEHAVING LIKE A LADY AND IF YOU THINK YOU ARE, YOU SHOULD SEE A PSYCHIATRIST. IF YOU ARE GOING TO CONTINUE TO SWEAR, YOU SHOULD LEAVE. I'LL GIVE YOU TWO WEEKS NOTICE".

Hmm, I thought, more threats about firing me. The writing was definitely on the wall. I wanted to remind him of how much he swore at me every day and how often I had heard Mrs. Cooke say things that would make the entire Redskins offensive line blush.

It had been an awful first day back from vacation. My idyllic week in Maine was already a distant memory. What the hell (oops, pardon the swear word) did he want from me? If he wanted me to be paranoid about my co-workers and not trust anyone, he had succeeded. I trusted no one now, especially the Kent Farms staff.

To top off the perfect day, Mr. Cooke called me after he returned home to Marbella about a message I had fax'd to him this morning. The message was not urgent, just a "touch base" sort of note. Apparently, neither he nor the houseman had checked the fax machine before he left for Redskin Park, so he didn't get the message until he returned home. Oh man, was he pissed (oops there I go swearing again). He wanted to know why I hadn't shown him the letter while he was at the Park. He hung up on me and then, after one minute, called back to continue his tirade. I reminded him it was normal procedure to fax messages to him at Marbella before he left for Redskin Park so he could read them during the drive. What I really wanted to say was "how was I supposed to know you didn't check your fax machine for messages this morning?!". It would have been be ridiculous to call him every time I faxed something to him, but I guessed I'd have to do that for a while, at least until he yelled at me to stop that too.

CHAPTER 99

Yes men

The No 1 requirement for anyone who worked for Mr. Cooke was that he or she be a "yes man". He was the king and NO ONE was to contradict him. That's why I found the following excerpt from a letter he had written to be so ironic.

> *"That I have had opinions which run counter to yours, is, in actual fact, beneficial to the NFL. 'Yes Men' generally forewarn a decline of virility in any organization. So, who cares that our psyches don't match. I don't. My convictions frequently find no residence in your mind (that's your prerogative), yet it's all to the good for all concerned."*

CHAPTER 100

Chew out du jour

It was a nice day at Redskin Park and Mr. Cooke and I were working outside on the patio when the shuttle arrived from Kent Farms. In the pouch was a check for Mrs. Cooke which required Mr. Cooke's signature. He picked up the check and put it in the accompanying envelope and, when he started to seal it, I stopped him and asked him if he had signed the check. He hadn't signed it and was grateful I had noticed. He signed the check, sealed the envelope (which was addressed to Mrs. Cooke at her Arlington address) and handed it to me and said "have it delivered today". I gave the envelope to the shuttle driver and told him to deliver it to Mrs. Cooke.

At 3:00 o'clock, Mr. Cooke called me from Marbella and yelled "WHAT HAVE YOU GONE AND DONE NOW? LOOK WHAT YOU'VE DONE. YOU'RE IN TROUBLE WITH ME ANYWAY, WOMAN! I TOLD YOU TO HAVE THAT CHECK SENT TO MARBELLA". I told him I did exactly what he told me to do and that was "have it delivered today"). He growled back at me "I'LL SEE YOU TOMORROW, YOUNG LADY".

I spent that night looking through the job ads.

CHAPTER 101

Thanks for all your effort and hard work

This week had been a real ball buster, more so than usual. Mr. Cooke had come in early every morning and stayed until 5:00 every night. It felt like I had been stuck in a swarm of bees the entire week. With his ceaseless buzzing and non-stop demands, I couldn't get anything accomplished. The big crisis this week had been a 50 page document on Mrs. Cooke's deportation issues, and he had an army of attorneys working on it.

Today, I had to listen to Mr. Cooke complain about some piddly, low priority thing I hadn't done yet. In self defense, I tried to remind him of the long hours I'd been working. I said "Well, sir, when it got to be 7:00 o'clock last night I went home". I shouldn't have been surprised by his apathetic response: "That doesn't matter, I work until 10 almost every night. So does my man in Los Angeles. So does my counsel". I bitterly laughed to myself and thought "yeah but I'm sure you don't pay yourself and them as poorly as me". I must have been crazy to think I could have gotten him to acknowledge all the extra hours I had been putting in. Outside of having the honor of being part of the Redskins organization and being able to attend games (I gave most of my tickets away because I preferred watching the games in the comfort of my own home or with friends), I got nothing out of this job except a lot of heartburn and stress. My salary was way below what it should have been and my "bonus" was getting my ass chewed on a regular basis.

CHAPTER 102

Lunch in DC with the team!

Much to my relief, Mr. Cooke stayed pretty quiet and spent most of the last week at Marbella. I was given a very special treat. I attended, along with all the other Redskins staff and players, the 32nd Annual Welcome Home Luncheon at the Omni Shoreham Hotel in DC, to honor the 1992 Super Bowl Champions. I felt the thrill of a little kid when I stepped out the front door of Redskin Park and saw three buses and several police cars and motorcycles. Our convoy had a police escort the entire way, from Redskin Park to the hotel! I rode in the first bus with the coaches and some of the players and, with eyes wide open with excitement, watched as the police cars and motorcycles, their red and blue lights flashing, guided us through red lights and busy intersections.

The buses had big banners on them and when we got into DC and onto its busy streets, people cheered when they saw us. I still couldn't believe I was part of it! The buses pulled up to the rear entrance of the hotel where we exited the buses and gathered into a "ready room" so the players and coaches could make their grand entrance. The rest of us made our way to our tables. After lunch and a couple of hours of awards and speeches, we hurried back onto the buses for our return to Redskin Park. It had been such a heady experience for me. I didn't think my feet would ever touch the ground again.

But soon enough, my feet came crashing to the ground. As if he wanted to make me pay for the incredible experience I had just had, Mr. Cooke was again turning up the heat and forcing me to work long hard hours. Since this was becoming a regular thing, I decided to try to get paid for overtime, like the rest of the Redskins staff did, or at least get some comp time. Unfortunately, when I asked, no one at Redskin Park seemed to know what to do, nor did anyone at Kent Farms.

I was caught in the middle, on my own planet with Mr. Cooke. And then I was afraid of what might happen if the Kent Farms manager told Mr. Cooke I had asked for overtime. I was sure he would be all put out and raise a big stink and remind me of what an honor it was to work for him. And then I would have to bite my tongue to keep from telling him that that great honor did not pay my bills and when was he going to give me a raise because it had been over 20 months! It was all a moot point, really, because I had pretty much given up and, with my two year anniversary with Mr. Cooke not far off, I knew I would be leaving soon. But it still frustrated the heck out of me.

Yesterday, at the Park, Mr. Cooke went all out to put on a show for one of his friends who was visiting. When the secretary of someone for whom Mr. Cooke had left a message returned his call, I buzzed him and told him "Miss X, secretary to Mr. X, is returning your call to Mr. X" and he took the call. As soon as he finished with the call, he buzzed me and, before I could even answer with my usual "yes sir?", he said, as fast as he could, "Mr. so and so was out of the office and therefore could not have returned my call" and slammed the phone down. What? Huh?

Also, yesterday, Mr. Cooke asked about the picture framer who was supposed to come to the Park to show him some samples. Two days before, the framer had to cancel, because his wife, who was also his business partner, was sick and needed to go in the hospital for some tests. He had told me he would call as soon as he could come up. So, I told Mr. Cooke I was waiting to hear from the framer and explained the situation. He threw his hands up in the air and said he'd find another framer, that he wanted some SERVICE! He never once considered the fact that this framer had provided many years of excellent and dependable service to the Redskins. But just like that, because the poor guy's wife was sick enough to cause a meeting to be delayed, he was ready to end the relationship. His heartless attitude reminded me of the old days in England when kings simply disposed of subjects who had displeased or inconvenienced them. Off with their heads!

CHAPTER 103

The suck up game

A note arrived at Redskin Park for Mr. Cooke. It had been written by one of his secretaries at Kent Farms to thank him for a "generous" raise. She had ended her note by telling Mr. Cooke that she loved her job and him.

OK . . . so where was MY raise? After I read this note, I thought to myself, "are we working for the same person?". I also thought that this was the biggest piece of BS that had ever been written. Talk about a suck up!

The note had said it all. If you played Mr. Cooke's game and kissed his 80 year old saggy ass, you got rewarded. I was no good at games. I had to be true to myself. There was no way I could play the "you're so wonderful, Mr. Cooke" game.

CHAPTER 104

Two weeks' notice

It was over for me, I was done. It was time to get out. I was only two months shy of my personal two-year goal and, all things considered, was very proud of myself for lasting as long as I did. The obstacles and challenges had been enormous. Through perseverance and just plain stubbornness, I had finally taught myself to stick it out and carry on and not take the easy way out by simply quitting and running away. Last night, I drafted my letter of resignation and this morning, I went into the office early, typed it up and put it on Mr. Cooke's desk. It read:

"Dear Mr. Cooke,

In keeping with our recent agreement, please consider this letter my two weeks' notice to you that I wish to resign as your executive secretary.

I have truly enjoyed working for the Redskins and wish you and I could have had a better and longer working relationship. But in light of our recent conversation and your frequent threats to fire me, I no longer feel secure in my position and therefore must take this most unfortunate step. I have made plans to relocate to New Jersey to be near my family. My last day in your employ will be Friday September 24.

I wish you the best of luck in all your ventures, especially in getting your new stadium built.

Sincerely,
Miss Crozier"

Mr. Cooke took my resignation very well, saying "I'm so sorry, we just weren't able to get along, were we? Well, it's just as much your fault as it is mine. Don't forget that".

A few minutes later, when I took a message in to him, he went on, saying it was "all for the better, that it was no secret we didn't get along, it was better for both of us and he'd 'give me a helluva reference'" which he dictated on the spot. After he finished the letter, he smiled at me and cheerfully said "how's that?". I said it was great and thanked him. He smiled at me again and said "you're okay, kid".

Our war was over. He had won.

CHAPTER 105

A new hood ornament for Mrs. Cooke's Jag

Two days after I resigned, Mrs. Cooke was again at the center of a major scandal. It was all over the news (both radio and TV) this morning that she had been picked up at 2:00 am in Georgetown for drunk driving and disorderly conduct. Splayed across the hood of her brand new Jaguar (which Mr. Cooke had just given her for her birthday), as she drove down M Street, was her 26 year old alleged lover, also feeling no pain.

Mrs. Cooke spent the night in jail. And all of this while she was fighting deportation! The INS was supposed to make its decision soon and Mr. Cooke had been doing everything possible to keep her from being deported. What a way to thank him, I thought.

I never saw Mr. Cooke again. On my last day at Redskin Park, everyone was so nice. Coaches, players and front office staff, a couple of them bearing autographed footballs, all stopped by to wish me luck.

When it was time to leave, I walked out the front door, got in my car, drove out through the security gate and never looked back. I was overcome with an incredible sense of relief and liberation. I also had a great sense of accomplishment at having remained Mr. Cooke's executive assistant for almost two years.

EPILOGUE

Shortly after I quit working for Mr. Cooke, I met my handsome, rich prince and we rode off into the sunset together on his beautiful white horse. . . NOT! It would be nice to say that happened, but it didn't. No prince. . . not even an ugly poor one. I did much better. I found myself.

I walked away from Mr. Cooke in full control of my life for the first time. I had graduated magna cum laude from Cooke University. I was as independent as the United States on the 4th of July. I was as fearless as the first woman who headed west into California on the Oregon Trail in her covered wagon. I was as confident as Nancy Pelosi the day she took the oath of office to become America's first female House Speaker. I was as strong and determined as Dianne Fossey with her beloved mountain gorillas. And I was tough: my skin was as thick as the bark of an ancient bristlecone pine tree. I would be in charge of my life from now on. And, just as important, I would still be that "too nice" person.

Ironically, prospective employers weren't sure how to react to my resume when they saw that I had been Jack Kent Cooke's executive assistant. Some thought me over qualified and that I'd be bored working in a "normal" office. Maybe they also sensed I was damaged goods. It was true, that after all the trauma I had suffered with Cooke, I had to teach myself all over again how to have normal conversations, that it was ok to ask someone how they were after they said hello, that it was okay to indulge in the usual social chit chat and make jokes and laugh and that I didn't have to run as fast as I could to the bathroom. There were a lot of ghosts I had to exorcise.

After a disappointing and unsuccessful job search in New Jersey, I returned to Virginia and did some "temp" work until I got a call from a head hunter about working for a "private individual" (oh no, again?). A little gun shy, but letting curiosity get the better of me, I pursued the opportunity and became personal assistant to Ethel Kennedy, widow of RFK. But, because I was unwilling to give up my home and move to the Kennedy Compound in Hyannis Port for 5 months every summer, I resigned after a few months.

Mr. Cooke died on April 6, 1997, at the age of 84. I was denied access to his funeral because the quaint Upperville, VA church was on the small side, and it had been more important for the media-worthy players, many of whom hadn't even known Mr. Cooke, to attend. So much for the faithful executive assistant who had spent hours at Mr. Cooke's bedside when he wasn't well and didn't want to be alone.

In the years that have followed, I have done things on my own that most women would never dream of doing, especially by themselves. I have traveled to remote and exotic islands on the other side of the world; I have scuba dived with 45 ft whale sharks in the Galapagos Islands, while surrounded by hundreds of schooling Hammerhead sharks; I have kayaked and fly fished in Alaska; I have hiked up New Hampshire's Mt. Washington into snow-packed Tuckerman's Ravine and skied back down. I have even been tear-gassed in front of the Presidential Palace in Quito, Ecuador (when I got too close to a student uprising). But I still haven't gone swimming in John's Bay!

Today, after 16+ years as executive assistant for the President & CEO and Board of Directors of the Natural Rural Telecommunications Cooperative in Herndon, Virginia, a wonderfully "normal" place staffed with friendly, caring people, I look forward to retiring soon and moving to Maine.

CPSIA information can be obtained at www.ICGtesting.com
Printed in the USA
268697BV00001B/31/P